MILITARY PSYCHOLOGY

Volume 18, Supplement, 2006

Special Issue:
Operational Psychology:
Training and Development Issues

Guest Editors:
Bjørn Helge Johnsen and Jarle Eid

(continued on next page)

MILITARY PSYCHOLOGY, 2006, *18*(Suppl.), S1–S2

PREFACE

Operational Psychology: Training and Development Issues

Bjørn Helge Johnsen and Jarle Eid
Department of Psychosocial Science
University of Bergen, Norway
and the Royal Norwegian Navy

Over the last decades, large-scale military operations have been characterized by multinational contributions. Troops from European nations have soldiered shoulder to shoulder with U.S. troops during the Balkan conflict, the war on terror in Afghanistan and Iraq, as well as in civilian emergencies like the tsunami relief efforts in south and east Asia. Thus, there is a growing need for more cross-cultural understanding to improve the execution of multinational operations. This supplement of *Military Psychology* is an attempt to fill a part of this knowledge gap.

The supplement reports on psychological factors that improve the readiness and execution of military operations. This could be termed *operational psychology*. Operational psychology is meant to generate empirical knowledge on individual and contextual factors influencing human behavior in dynamic settings that produce a hazard to life, health, or basic values.

The issue, "Operational Psychology: Training and Developmental Issues," explores new empirical research focusing on the training and education of personnel and leaders of operational units. The following three aspects of operational psychology are addressed: training, education of leaders, and conducting operations. Training issues are addressed by two articles, in which factors enhancing individual (Saus et al.) and team performance (Espevik, Johnsen, Eid, & Thayer) are investigated using modern simulators. Educational issues are covered by five articles

Correspondence should be addressed to Bjørn Helge Johnsen, Department of Psychosocial Science, University of Bergen, Christiesgt. 12, 5015 Bergen, Norway. E-mail: bjoern.johnsen@psysp.uib.no

describing different aspects of leader development. Two studies focus on education of officer cadets. In one study the individual level of moral development is seen a predictor of transformational leadership (Olsen, Eid, & Johnsen), and in another study, West Point cadets, U.S. civilians, and cadets from the Royal Norwegian Naval Academy are compared on character strengths and virtues (Matthews, Eid, Kelly, Bailey, & Peterson). The cross-cultural aspect of junior officer training is further investigated in a study aimed at describing factors involved in leader development across five different nations (Larsson et al.). Late career development is covered by a study on significant factors involved in being promoted to Flag officer (Schwind & Laurence). Finally, the education part consists of a brief report on the implementation of a leadership development program in the Swedish Armed Forces (Larsson). To train and educate soldiers, sailors, and air force personnel, experiences from operations and critical incidents have to be analyzed and fed back into the organization. This issue presents two articles with that focus. Based on accident reports, one study investigates navigation accidents in the Royal Norwegian Navy (Gould, Røed, Koefoed, Bridger, & Moen). In the final article Bartone addresses the potential of influencing resilience by developing personality hardiness in operational personnel. Both studies present and discuss empirical findings that could influence training and education to improve the execution of operations.

ACKNOWLEDGMENTS

We would like to acknowledge support from the Royal Norwegian Ministry of Defence, the University of Bergen, Norway, the Norwegian Naval Medical Service, and the Royal Norwegian Naval Academy in producing this supplement of *Military Psychology*.

MILITARY PSYCHOLOGY, 2006, *18*(Suppl.), S3–S21

TRAINING

The Effect of Brief Situational Awareness Training in a Police Shooting Simulator: An Experimental Study

Evelyn-Rose Saus
Department of Psychosocial Science
University of Bergen, Norway

Bjørn Helge Johnsen and Jarle Eid
Department of Psychosocial Science
University of Bergen, Norway
and the Royal Norwegian Navy

Per Ketil Riisem and Rune Andersen
Department of Education
The Norwegian Police University College
Oslo, Norway

Julian F. Thayer
Department of Health Psychology
The Ohio State University

The aim of this study was to investigate the effect of situational awareness (SA) training in a shooting simulator. Forty 1st-year students from the Norwegian Police University College participated in this study. They were divided into 2 groups and matched with respect to sex and previous weapon experience. The SA-trained group received scenario-based training with freeze technique and reflection based on the

Correspondence should be addressed to Evelyn-Rose Saus, Department of Psychosocial Science, University of Bergen, Christiesgt. 12, 5015 Bergen, Norway. E-mail: evelyn-rose.saus@psysp.uib.no

SA stages, whereas the control group received skill training. During the test phase SA was measured both subjectively and objectively and performance was measured by the number of shots fired and number of hits. The results showed that both subjective and observer ratings reported the SA-trained group to have higher SA. This was also true for performance, and the SA-trained group showed less mental workload measured as suppression of heart rate variability during the execution of the mission. These results indicate that brief SA-specific training in a shoot–not shoot simulator can improve police cadets' SA in critical situations.

There is increased international focus on the use of force in modern police work. In particular, the use of weapons to control critical situations has been heavily debated in the media. Situations involving the use of firearms are often characterized by a rapidly evolving scenario, complex environment, a great deal of uncertainty, and a high degree of fear. For a police officer these factors make it extremely difficult to decide whether or not to shoot. Such demanding situations take a heavy toll on the mental capacity of the police officer, and the same factors can be identified in military operations. Thus, a need for experimental studies on methods of education and training of military populations and police officers has evolved.

One critical factor in making adequate decisions in critical situations is generating and maintaining *situational awareness* (SA; Endsley, 1999; Klein, 2000). SA refers to cognitive processes involved in perceiving and comprehending the meaning of a given environment. SA, in turn, enhances the capacity to make timely and effective decisions. A core element in these decisions is ability to project likely events in the near future (Matthews, Strater, & Endsley, 2004). Thus, SA is a conscious dynamic reflection of the situation, and its reflects the past, present, and future. Endsley (1988) proposed a three-stage model for SA, with each stage being a necessary (but not sufficient) precursor to the next level. The first level involves the fundamental perception of the elements of a particular environment. Further the officer has to understand the meaning of the percepted elements. This comprehension involves the second stage in the model, and the last stage represents the projection of future events. During a mission it is important for the police officer to be aware of the surroundings, like numbers of civilians and if there are any casualties. Based on this information the police officer might expect further events, such as a perpetrator with a weapon. This again will have implications for the officer's decision making.

SA is closely linked to human decision making and performance, and can be critical to effective functioning in complex and dynamic environments (Endsley & Garland, 2000; Matthews et al., 2004). Svensson and Wilson (2002) showed that mission complexity affects workload, which affects both SA and performance. This link is often reported in aviation accidents resulting from inadequate situational assessment and SA (Garland, Wise, & Hopkin, 1999; Shebilske, Goettl, &

Garland, 2000). Studies of SA have also been conducted in environments like air traffic control rooms and different military settings (Matthews et al., 2004; Rodgers, Mogford, & Strauch, 2000). The profusion of information technology results in an increased cognitive workload. At the same time the environment can be constantly changing, giving rise to unexpected events (Matthews et al., 2004; Rodgers et al., 2000).

Research has documented SA's fundamental role in skilled performance (Endsley & Bolstad, 1994; Endsley & Kaber, 1999). SA training may address both individual and team-level processes and behaviors. Both the use of simulators and training are interventions aimed at improving performance.

Today there are relatively few empirical outcome evaluations of SA training programs. One of the reasons is the focus on SA-oriented design and automation issues. Beyond automation, effective training can be achieved by improving the skills and knowledge critical for achieving good SA. Factors in individual training may involve higher order cognitive skills training, intensive briefings, use of structured feedback, and SA-oriented training programs, such as information seeking and training specifically focused to develop SA and decision making (see Endsley & Robertson, 2000, for an overview). Individual training should aim at improving critical information-seeking and information-processing behaviors (Salas, Prince, Baker, & Shrestha, 1995). This can be done by systematically exposing the individual to different scenarios with guided practice and feedback. For example, on a team level, Salas et al. (1995) recommended that SA training should focus on complex communication behaviors, team planning, and task-specific competencies, such as roles and position in the team.

Because there are few empirical studies on the effects of SA training, there is a need to empirically evaluate specific SA training techniques. One promising technique is the so-called freeze technique (Endsley, 1995). This technique involves stopping or "freezing" a simulated operational task at randomly chosen points in time. Queries are then made concerning the three levels of SA. This technique is largely nonintrusive and gives a good understanding of the individual's SA, which again gives a more accurate measure of SA. Romano and Brna (2001) suggested that to improve performance, training must also offer the opportunity to reflect on one's performance. Thus, by combining the freeze technique and reflection about a specific scenario one could study the effect of scenario-based SA training (Endsley, 1988).

One way to train SA is by the use of simulators. The use of simulation has become an important technology for skills training. Simulators can provide a safe learning environment and are regarded as a cost-effective training regime (White, Carson, & Wilbourn, 1991b). The scientific advantage of using simulators involves thorough control of the setting and the capacity to systematically manipulate training variables; for example, individuals can train under different levels of stress, time pressure, and workload. Virtual reality allows the presence of this type of experimental control, and at the same time involves a high level of realism in the scenarios; such realism further increases generalizability of the results.

For police, lethal and nonlethal force are essential components in preparation for future violent confrontations. Such high-risk encounters are relatively infrequent field events that are difficult to examine in a natural setting. A simulator affords the possibility to study police shooting behavior in a controlled setting and may provide insight into the use of lethal force in the field.

SA as a theoretical concept involves basic cognitive processes like attention, perception, and decision making. A core element in these processes is the use of executive functions (Baddeley, 1986). Executive functions are responsible for human planning, reasoning, problem solving, decision making, and acting. Different aspects of executive control involve selecting, maintaining, updating, and rerouting of information (Shimamura, 2000). Thus, executive functions can be said to be basic processes in SA, and especially salient at levels two (perception of a situation) and three (projection in the near future).

Recent studies in our research group demonstrate a relation between individual differences in heart rate variability (HRV), as an index of neurovisceral integration (see Thayer & Lane, 2000), and executive function on continuous performance and working memory tasks (Hansen, Johnsen, Sollers, Stenvik, & Thayer, 2004; Hansen, Johnsen, & Thayer, 2003). Those individuals with greater HRV performed better on executive function tasks and better under conditions of threat (Hansen et al., 2003). Given the relation between SA and executive function, measures of individual differences in HRV may be useful in the understanding of SA. Based on our laboratory studies we would expect those persons with greater HRV to also show greater SA. Extending these findings to a simulation would offer an important generalization of our laboratory findings to a real-life situation and could have important implications for selection and training.

In addition, HRV is a promising dependent variable in studies of workload and cognitive demand. In response to increasing workload and cognitive demand, measures of vagally mediated HRV are reduced in a dose-dependent manner (Fairclough, Venables, & Tattersall, 2005). Increased load on working memory is associated with mental effort. It is therefore possible to use HRV as an indicator of mental effort (Backs & Seljos, 1994), where it is expected that HRV decreases as mental effort increases (Meshkati, 1988). Magnusson (2002) indicated that a pilot's psychophysiological reactions in the simulator are similar to those in real flight, and that HRV is expected to decrease as mental effort increases. It is therefore possible to examine HRV in two distinct ways: (a) as an individual difference variable that may be related to SA, and (b) as a dependent variable that may index task demands and the interaction of task demands and individual differences.

The aim of this study was to investigate the effect of SA training in a shooting simulator. It was predicted that a group receiving scenario-based training combined with reflection on the SA stages would report higher SA and subjective learning effects compared to a control group receiving skill training. Importantly, this training effect should also be reflected in observer ratings of SA. In addition, it has been suggested that SA is associated with improved performance and thus we predicted improved performance as indicated by a higher number of shots fired and more hits for the SA-trained group. Firing more is not always a good indicator of high SA. In this study this was done because the test scenario involved a setting where successful performance required participants to fire their weapon, and the firearms training simulator (FATS) did not stop the scenarios until a fatal shot was fired. Therefore, number of shots fired was used as a performance measure. Furthermore, the relations among SA, executive function, and HRV suggest that those persons with greater HRV would show evidence of greater SA. Finally, because SA has been related to the concept of mental workload, and HRV has been used as a measure of workload, we predicted that the SA-trained group would show less suppression of HRV during the execution of the mission compared to the control group.

METHOD

Participants

A total of 40 students (20 men and 20 women) from the first year of training at the Norwegian Police University College participated in the study. The mean age was 24.88 years (range = 20–33). The Police University College is a 3-year program that includes theoretical and practical courses related to modern policing. Sex, age, and previous experience with weapons were also recorded.

Apparatus and Questionnaires

Data were collected during mission training in a shoot–not shoot simulator (FATS). The simulator was situated in a room of 70 m^2, with a computerized movie projector and standard service weapons, retrofitted with a laser-emitting device to mark the impact of the weapon. The simulator used gas (CO_2) to simulate weapon recoil, and had noise-report capability. Although the simulator is set up for several weapons, this study only used the MP5 (Heckler & Kock) as a weapon. The computer displayed realistic video-based simulated scenarios designed to test the student's judgment and skill in the use of deadly force under stressful conditions. The system registered movements of the weapon, number of shots fired, and the effect of each bullet and point of impact.

Cardiovascular responses were recorded using an ambulatory monitoring system (AMS; Klaver, de Geus, & de Vries, 1994). The cardiac responses were measured using 1 cm Ag/AgCl ECG electrodes (Ultratrace, disposable pregelled electrodes). One electrode was placed over the jugular notch of the sternum, between the collarbones, another was placed 4 cm under the left breast between the ribs, and the third electrode was placed at the right lateral side between the two lower ribs.

SA was measured using two different self-report questionnaires, both translated into Norwegian. The first questionnaire was the Situational Awareness Rating Scale (SARS; Waag & Houck, 1994, adapted for use in a shooting simulator). The Norwegian version consisted of 25 items (scored 1–6) concerning general traits, and the SA dimensions of tactical planning, system operations, communication, information interpretation, tactical decisions, and general tactic (see also Dalseg, 2000). An example of a general trait item was "I have good knowledge about shooting." An example SA item was "To what extent could you create a mental model of the situation?" In a pilot study an internal consistency of .86 was found (Dalseg & Johnsen, 2001). The second SA scale was the Situational Awareness Behaviorally Anchored Rating Scale (SABARS). This questionnaire was a direct subjective measure of SA, which was also utilized with expert-observer rating on behaviors linked to SA in the specific context (Matthews, Beal, & Pleban, 2001). The instrument consisted of 18 items divided into three dimensions: the participant's awareness of own SA (e.g., "To what extent did you know your own resources?"), awareness of the perpetrator (e.g., "To what extent did you know the perpetrator's placement?"), and the awareness of the mission (e.g., "To what extent did you understand possible obstacles in performing your mission?").

Both the SARS and the SABARS were administered in a subjective rating version and an observer rating version. The SARS observer rating version consisted of the 15 SA items only. The general trait items were excluded. Because the SABARS questionnaire was behaviorally anchored, the observer rating version consisted of the same 18 items as the subjective rating version.

In addition, the participants were asked two questions about learning and realism in the situation (e.g., "To what extent did you learn from the experience?"; scored 1–6) as well as four questions about training effects on decision making involved in handling a critical situation involving weapon use (e.g., "To what extent has the training given you an increased understanding of the rules and regulations of weapon use?"; scored 1–6).

Procedure

Before the start of the experiment, participants read and signed an informed consent statement. They were informed about their right to leave the experiment at any time. No participants withdrew from the experiment. All were tested individually in the simulator at the Norwegian Police University College.

The participants were matched with respect to sex and previous experience using weapons, and then randomly assigned to either the test (SA-trained) or the control (skill-only) group. Both the SA-trained group and the control group consisted of 20 participants.

This study consisted of two phases. During the training phase, the SA-trained group received scenario-based training in the simulator. The participants were armed with an MP5 during all sessions and each of the three sessions involved different missions in which the police might have to use the weapon, and others in which the preferred action was not to use a weapon. Every scenario involved a freeze technique, where the video was stopped and the participants were asked questions related to Endsley's (1988) three levels of SA. During debriefing, after each session, participants were encouraged to reflect on the levels of SA and relate the scenarios to the rules and regulations of the use of weapons in the police force.

In the training phase, the control group got general information about the use of the simulator and practiced the use of MP5. The sessions consisted of training in marksmanship skills. Each target practice consisted of three different exercises with different targets, selection of targets, and permanent and mobile targets. The control group was asked to reflect on the rules and regulation of the use of weapons in the police force. The training sessions involved increased degree of difficulty. Time spent in the simulator as well as the number of sessions were identical for the two groups.

The test phase consisted of a simulated scenario for all the participants. After HRV electrodes were placed on the participants, the sequence of 5 min of baseline, preparing for the mission, the execution of the operation, and 5 min of recovery was performed on all participants. Suppression of vagal activity was used as an indication of workload. Vagal activity was measured as the root mean of the squared successive differences (HRV). This index of vagal innervations of the heart correlates highly (.90) with spectral derived indexes of parasympathetic drive to the heart (Hayano et al., 1991), and the suppression of HRV is frequently used as a measure of strain to the organism.

When preparing for the mission (preparation phase) the operational leader informed participants about the mission, and participants got the opportunity to ask questions concerning the mission. They also had time to prepare their weapon, protective gear, and radio. Then they completed the mission with freezing sessions that included questions about SA. Freeze sessions allowed the observer to evaluate participants' SA levels.

SA data were collected by having the respondents fill in the self-report SA questionnaires. For the self-report SARS, nine summary scores were produced. These included a total summary score, which was the sum of all 25 items; the sum score of the 15 SA items only; and 7 dimension scores. In addition, sum scores of the learning and realism questions, as well as sum scores of effect of training on decision making were constructed for each participant. An expert observer was used to obtain external ratings of SA. The expert was an instructor in tactical weapon use recruited from the other Police University College in Norway. The observer had no information regarding which of the participants were exposed to which conditions. The observer's SARS rating was based on a summary score of the 15 SA items. For both the subjective and observer SABARS versions, the sum score for all 18 items was used, and there were also three sum scores for each of the dimensions.

Performance was measured by number of shots fired and number of hits. This was done because the test scenario involved a setting in which successful performance required participants to fire their weapon. The FATS did not stop the scenarios until a fatal shot was fired. Therefore, number of shots fired was used as a performance measure. The experiment ended with a mission debriefing from both the operational leader and the observer.

Design and Statistics

An independent group design with matched random assignment was used (Cozby, 1993). T tests for independent samples were used to investigate differences between the two groups regarding SA and performance. The results were also based on one-tailed tests due to the hypothesized direction of the means (Ferguson, 1981). Differences in HRV were tested by using a 2 (SA-trained vs. control group) × 4 (baseline vs. preparing vs. execution vs. recovery) analysis of variance (ANOVA). The first factor was treated as a between-group factor and the second as a within-groups factor. The relation among cardiovascular responses, SA levels, and outcome measures were investigated using Pearson product–moment correlation.

RESULTS

Reliability Analyses

Analyses of the questionnaires showed a Cronbach's alpha on the 25-item SARS of .85 (external ratings = .96). The Cronbach's alpha of the SABARS was .78 (external ratings = .89). The four items concerning decision making in critical situations revealed a Cronbach's alpha of .68.

Effects of SA Training on Subjective Measures of SA

Analyses of the SARS questionnaire showed a higher level of subjective SA for the SA-trained group compared to the control group, $t(37) = -1.89, p < .05$. This was the case for the sum score on SA items only (see Figure 1). When separating the SARS into the dimensions, a higher SA level was found in the trained group compared to the control group on tactical decision making, $t(37) = -2.14, p < .05$, and general tactics, $t(37) = -2.31, p < .05$.

On the SABARS questionnaire, higher scores were found on the dimension concerning awareness of the perpetrator, $t(35) = -1.75, p < 05$, for the SA-trained group (Figure 1). No other comparisons were significant.

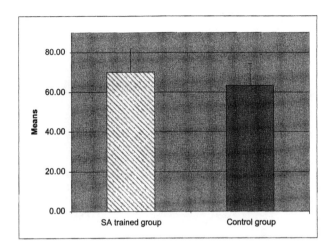

FIGURE 1   Mean sum score of the SARS questionnaire (SA items only). The scores are based on subjective rating and are separated for SA-trained group and control group.

Effects of SA Training on Observer Ratings

Figure 2 presents mean sum scores on observer ratings of SA. For the SARS summary score there was a significant difference between the groups, $t(38) = -3.52$, $p < .01$, in which the observer reported a higher level of SA in the SA-trained group.

The observer ratings on the SABARS summary score, $t(33) = -2.65$, $p < .01$, showed a higher level of SA in the SA-trained group. The observer also reported higher SA levels in the SA-trained group compared to the control group on all the

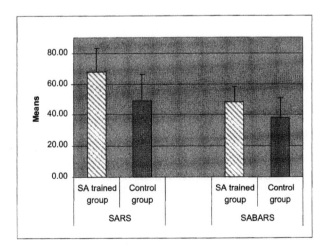

FIGURE 2   Mean sum score of the SARS and SABARS questionnaires. The scores are based on observer rating and are separated for SA-trained group and control group.

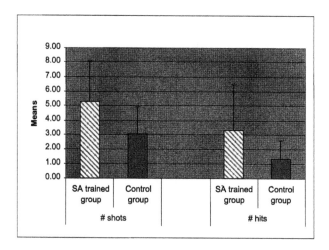

FIGURE 3   Mean sum score of performance measures. The scores are based on number of shots fired and number of hits on target, and are separated for SA-trained group and control group.

subdimensions of SABARS: awareness of own situation, $t(33) = -2.84$, $p < .01$; awareness of the perpetrator, $t(33) = -1.94$, $p < .05$; and awareness of the mission, $t(33) = -2.54$, $p < .05$.

Performance Measures

The SA-trained group fired more shots, $t(34) = -2.82$, $p < .01$, and had a higher number of hits on target, $t(34) = -2.51$, $p < .05$, compared to the control group (see Figure 3).

Learning and Training Effects on Decision Making

The SA-trained group showed higher self-ratings of decision making involved in handling a critical situation, $t(37) = -1.85$, $p < .05$, compared to the control group. No other significant effects were found.

Cardiovascular Responses

Correlations between HRV during the four phases and SA measures were performed. As predicted, analyses showed a positive correlation between SA scores (SA items only) and HRV measured during the HRV preparation phase, $r(40) = .39$, $p < .01$. In addition, borderline correlations were found between HRV measured during the baseline and execution phases and SA scores on the SARS, $r(40) = .25$, $p < .06$, and $r(40) = .23$, $p < .07$, respectively. The same pattern occurred when using the total score on the SARS. Positive correlations were found between

SARS total and baseline measures of HRV, $r(40) = .27, p < .05$; recordings during the preparation phase, $r(40) = .43, p < .01$; as well as during the execution phase, $r(40) = .29, p < .04$. Significant correlations were also found between ratings of learning from the experience and HRV measured at baseline, $r(40) = .30, p < .03$ (one-tailed); during the preparation phase, $r(40) = .42, p < .01$; as well as during the execution phase, $r(40) = .32, p < .05$.

To investigate the effects of workload and cognitive demand, a Group (2 levels: SA-trained vs. control) × Experimental Phase (4 levels: baseline, preparation, execution, and recovery) ANOVA was performed. A main effect of the phase was found on the HRV data, $F(1, 3) = 11.7, p < .01$. A least significant different post hoc test showed a suppression of HRV from baseline to the preparation phase ($p < .01$). There was a further suppression of HRV from the preparation phase to the execution phase ($p < .03$), followed by a significant increase in HRV in the recovery phase ($p < .01$). To follow up a possible differential effect on the cardiovascular reactivity between the two groups, preplanned simple effects tests were used (Wilcox, 1987). The t tests revealed that the SA-trained group did not show suppression of HRV from the preparation phase to the execution phase. This was in contrast to the control group, which showed this suppression of HRV from preparation through to the execution of the mission ($p < .05$).

Subjective Versus Observational Ratings of SA and Learning

Table 1 shows correlations between self-report measures of SA, observer measures of SA, and scores on subjective experience of learning, as well as effect on decision making in critical situations. As can be seen in Table 1, strong correlations were found between self-report and observer ratings of SA (all $p < .01$). Learning and decision making were not correlated to external ratings of SA. Further analyses showed that self-report ratings of SA were positively related to subjective feeling of learning: SARS total, $r(40) = .31, p < .05$; SA items only, $r(40) = .31, p < .05$; and the sum score SABARS, $r(37) = .37, p < .03$. Self-report subjective ratings of SABARS were borderline related to effect on decision making, $r(36) = .26, p < .06$.

SA Ratings and Performance

Tables 2 and 3 show Pearson product–moment correlations between self-report and observer ratings of SA and number of shots fired and number of hits on target. The tables show that both SA questionnaires and their subdimensions showed positive significant correlations with the number of shots fired. The only exceptions were the communication dimension on the SARS and awareness of the mission on the SABARS. Positive correlations between SA measures and number of hits were found on the sum scores of SA items only (one-tailed) and on the SARS total, as

TABLE 1
Correlation Analysis for Subjective Versus Observational Ratings of SA
and Learning

Subjective SA	Observer Ratings				
	SARS	Sum SABARS	Own	Perpetrator	Mission
SARS total	.53**	.48**	.44**	.28	.57**
SA items only	.54**	.48**	.44**	.29*	.57**
Sum SABARS	.40**	.43**	.34*	.26	.53**
Own	.29*	.26	.20	.12	.38*
Perpetrator	.38*	.45**	.40**	.29*	.51**
Mission	.25	.32*	.17	.23	.40**
Learning	.11	.05	.17	−.03	.09
Decision making	−.02	.17	.22	.12	.10

Note. $N = 40$. The table is separated in sum scores for SARS total and SA items only, sum score SABARS, and three dimensions: participant's own awareness (own), awareness of the perpetrator (perpetrator), and awareness of the mission (mission). SA = situational awareness; SARS = Situational Awareness Rating Scale; SABARS = Situational Awareness Behaviorally Anchored Rating Scale.
   *$p < .05$. **$p < .001$.

TABLE 2
Correlation Analysis Between Subjective Ratings of SA and Performance

Subjective SA Ratings	Shots	Hits
SARS total	.62**	.34*
SARS SA items only	.58**	.27*
General trait	.50**	.40**
Tactical planning	.52**	.19
System operations	.38*	.16
Communication	.10	.14
Information interpretation	.48**	.16
Tactical decision	.60**	.31*
General tactic	.34*	.28*
Sum SABARS	.39*	.23
Own	.34*	.23
Perpetrator	.33*	.11
Mission	.21	.17

Note. $N = 40$. The SARS data are separated in sum scores for SARS total and SA items only. SA items only are further separated for the seven dimensions. The SABARS data are divided in sum score SABARS and the three dimensions: participant's own awareness (own), awareness of the perpetrator (perpetrator), and awareness of the mission (mission). Performance data are presented as mean number of shots fired (shots) and number of hits on target (hits). Correlation analysis for observer ratings of SA and performance measured in number of shots fired (shots) and number of hits on target (hits). SA = situational awareness; SARS = Situational Awareness Rating Scale; SABARS = Situational Awareness Behaviorally Anchored Rating Scale.
   *$p < .05$. **$p < .001$.

TABLE 3
Correlation Analysis Between Observer Ratings of SA and Performance

Observer Ratings of SA	Shots	Hits
Sum SARS	.50**	.46**
Sum SABARS	.46**	.34
Own	.46**	.36*
Perpetrator	.33*	.26
Mission	.45**	.37*

Note. $N = 40$. The SARS data are separated in sum scores for SARS total. The SABARS data are divided in sum score SABARS and the three dimensions: participant's own awareness (own), awareness of the perpetrator (perpetrator), and awareness of the mission (mission). Performance data are presented as mean number of shots fired (shots) and number of hits on target (hits). Correlation analysis for observer ratings of SA and performance measured in number of shots fired (shots) and number of hits on target (hits). SA = situational awareness; SARS = Situational Awareness Rating Scale; SABARS = Situational Awareness Behaviorally Anchored Rating Scale.
*$p < .05$. **$p < .001$.

well as the dimensions of general trait, tactical decision (one-tailed), and general tactics (one-tailed). Observer ratings showed a positive relation between both SARS and SABARS scores and number of hits on target (see Tables 2 and 3 for details).

DISCUSSION

The results of this study showed that the SA-trained group reported a higher level of subjective SA and decision making during a critical situation compared to the control group. Subjective ratings were confirmed by observer ratings. Furthermore, performance data showed that the SA-trained group recorded both a higher number of shots fired and a greater number of hits on target compared to the control group. Further analyses examined individual differences in SA and revealed positive correlations between SA as measured by both self-report and observers, and performance as indexed by number of shots fired and number of hits. The results also suggested that individual differences in HRV were associated with SA such that, consistent with our predictions, persons with higher resting HRV had higher SA. Finally, the results supported the predicted relation between task demands and HRV such that HRV decreased during the performance of the task but did so less for the SA-trained group.

The first aim of the study was to investigate the effect of SA training in a shooting simulator, where it was hypothesized that the SA-trained group would report higher levels of SA. It was expected that the SA training would increase SA and thus could develop comprehension, judgment concerning risk level, and better projection of future events. The latter could be important in unexpected and critical situations. This is in line with Orasanu, Dismukes, and Fischer (1993), who reported that experienced pilots appeared to spend time preflight planning, seeking information in advance, and data gathering. These actions can reduce workload in critical events, and are important for good SA. SA training can also facilitate construction of mental models, which are an important precursor for good SA (Endsley & Robertson, 2000).

We also expected higher SA for the SA-trained group because the training consisted of both shoot and not shoot scenarios and thorough debriefing with a focus on the participants' decision making and understanding of the situation (Salas et al., 1995). As predicted, participants reported higher subjective SA on the sum score of the 15 SARS SA items. This result was also supported by the behaviorally anchored questionnaire (SABARS), on the awareness of the perpetrator dimension. Of course, a possible explanation can be that the SA-trained group members had their main focus on the perpetrator because the purpose of the mission was to identify and act against the perpetrator. It could also be that the SARS and SABARS measure distinct factors in SA. SARS combines assessment on many dimensions, including decision-making abilities, skills, and performance (Jones, 2000), whereas SABARS is directly linked to SA through relevant behavior.

This study created significant differences between the SA-trained and the control group in only three sessions. The use of both the freezing technique and reflection may have resulted in better opportunity to efficiently acquire knowledge and experience, which resulted in rapid improvement in SA. Experience can reduce the amount of resources required for specific tasks, which may result in more resources available for achieving SA (Endsley & Bolstad, 1994). These factors are also important in decision making, and there was also a difference between the groups concerning decision making in handling a critical situation. Again the SA-trained group reported higher ratings compared to the control group. Romano and Brna (2001) claimed that when training limited decision-making skills, there should be opportunity to reflect on actions and strategies to improve performance. Thus training in virtual environments should provide both skills and reflection. The results from this study support this suggestion.

In this study the participants were first-year students at the Norwegian Police University College and novices with regard to simulator training. It is possible that the effects seen here only occur among novices. Such an argument was forwarded by White et al. (1991b), who claimed that a trainer was effective for teaching marksmanship skills for those with minimal weapon expertise. Buffardi and Allen (1986) also concluded that high-fidelity simulators enhance the performance of low-ability students more than high-ability students. Future research should consider whether simulator training is valuable for experts in terms of performance and SA (White, Carson, & Wilbourn, 1991a).

In the literature there has been discussion of whether to use self-report or objective ratings of SA (Vidulich, Stratton, Crabtree, & Wilson, 1994). The high correlations between observer and self-report ratings support the use of self-report ratings in studies of factors influencing SA. However, the use of both self-report and observer ratings may give a more accurate measure of SA.

This study also predicted that the SA-trained group would perform better than the control group. Both the self-report and the observer ratings showed that this was true both for number of shots fired and number of hits. The positive correlations between self-reported SA and number of shots fired might be explained by the technical construction of the shooting simulator. It is constructed in such a way that the perpetrator does not fall and stop shooting unless he or she is hit by a lethal shot. It could be that the participants observed this, and fired more shots and had a higher number of hits because they were able to monitor when the threat was eliminated. Because of their higher SA, participants in the SA-trained group focused on the perpetrator and managed to fire more shots when the perpetrator opened fire. This is further supported by the fact that the SA-trained group reported higher SA on the awareness of the perpetrator dimension. These clear indications from both self-report and observer ratings support the notion that SA training leads to increased SA and subsequently to increased performance.

There was also evidence for individual differences in SA independent of training. Analyses revealed a positive correlation between the SA questionnaires and performance. This finding is in accordance with Svensson and Wilson (2002), whose model analysis showed a positive correlation between SA and performance. Also Svensson, AngelborgThanderz, Sjoberg, and Olsson (1997) found positive correlation between performance in a flight task and SA. The results also give support to Endsley and Garland (2000), who emphasized high SA as an important factor for successful performance.

Individual differences in HRV were also found to be related to SA. This represents an important extension of laboratory-based studies in which persons with higher HRV performed better on tasks that tapped executive functioning (Hansen et al., 2004; Hansen et al., 2003). Given the literature suggesting that executive functioning is critical to SA, particularly the latter two stages, these results provide a real-world validation of our previous findings and suggest that individual differences in HRV could have important practical implications for performance of mission in critical tasks. The highest positive correlation was found between HRV recorded during preparation for the mission and self-reported SA. During the preparation phase the participants received the description of and orders for the mission. This could lead to an increase in mental effort and anxiety. Because mental effort and anxiety have been closely related to HRV (Thayer, Friedman, & Borkovec, 1996), it could explain why the effect was most dominant in this phase. A similar pattern was found for the relation between HRV and learning. Because learning also would rely on executive functioning, the previous reported link between HRV and executive functioning could explain these results. Further research will be necessary to explicate the consequences of these findings for selection and training. However, given that HRV can be manipulated via, for example, physical exercise with concomitant changes in performance, it may be possible to combine SA training with physical fitness training to optimize performance of mission personnel.

The results with respect to changes in HRV as a function of cognitive demand, and the relatively lesser impact as indexed by less HRV suppression during the execution phase of the simulator task in the SA-trained group also suggest ways in which SA training and training to increase HRV might be usefully combined. For example, our previous work has shown that persons with higher HRV were more stress tolerant and showed a smaller cortisol response to cognitive challenge (Johnsen, Hansen, Sollers, Murison, & Thayer, 2002). Cortisol has been shown to decrease performance on executive function tasks and thus provides one pathway by which increased SA and the attendant increased HRV and decreased cortisol response could work to buffer individuals from the adverse effects of cognitive demand.

The positive relation between SA and performance may also be evidence of the validity of our measures of SA. Results from this study showed that both the self-report and observer SA questionnaires capture expected differences and relations with performance. This gives an indication of validity of the questionnaires used (Johnsen & Hugdahl, 1990). The questionnaires also showed acceptable reliability indicated by Cronbach's alpha for self-report ratings of SARS and SABARS. The alpha values were .78 and .85, respectively.

In summary, this study showed that brief SA-specific training in a shoot–not shoot simulator improved police cadets' SA. This was the case for both self-report and observer ratings. SA-specific training also resulted in increased performance. The SA training was superior to the skill training in the simulator because previous experience was matched in the two groups. The only difference was that one group conducted skill training (marksmanship) and the other group was involved in scenario-based SA-specific training using freeze techniques and reflection based on the SA stages. The finding that HRV was related to SA opens several potentially interesting lines of investigation with respect to selection and training. Future work is needed to illuminate the mechanisms responsible for these effects and how they might be utilized in the service of improved performance in critical situations.

REFERENCES

Backs, R. W., & Seljos, K. A. (1994). Metabolic and cardio respiratory measures of mental effort: The effects of level of difficulty in working memory task. *International Journal of Psychophysiology, 16,* 5–68.

Baddeley, A. D. (1986). *Working memory.* Oxford, England: Oxford University Press.

Buffardi, L. C., & Allen, J. A. (1986, June). *Simulator fidelity and individual differences: An aptitude-treatment interaction.* Paper presented at the first midyear conference of the Society of Industrial and Organizational Psychology, Chicago.

Cozby, P. C. (1993). *Methods in behavioral research* (7th ed.). Mountain View, CA: Mayfield.

Dalseg, B. K. (2000). *Effekten av ulike navigasjonssimulatorer på situasjonsbevissthet og kardiovaskulær aktivitet* [The effect of different navigation simulators on situational awareness and cardiovascular activity]. Unpublished master's thesis, University of Bergen, Norway.

Dalseg, B. K., & Johnsen, B. H. (2001). *Psykometriske mål på situasjonsbevissthet* [Psychometric measures of situational awareness] (Research Rep. 6, Military psychology and leadership). Bergen, Norway: Royal Norwegian Naval Academy.

Endsley, M. R. (1988). Design and evaluation for situation awareness enhancement. In *Proceedings of the Human Factors Society 32nd Annual Meeting* (pp. 97–101). Santa Monica, CA: Human Factors Society.

Endsley, M. R. (1995). Measurement of situation awareness in dynamic systems. *Human Factors, 37,* 65–84.

Endsley, M. R. (1999). Situation awareness and human error: Designing to support human performance. In *Proceedings of the High Consequence System Surety Conference.* Albuquerque, NM: Sandia National Laboratory.

Endsley, M. R., & Bolstad, C. A. (1994). Individual differences in pilot situation awareness. *International Journal of Aviation Psychology, 4,* 241–264.

Endsley, M. R., & Garland, D. J. (2000). Pilot situation awareness training in general aviation. In *Proceedings of the 14th Triennial Congress of the International Ergonomics Association and the 44th Annual Meeting of the Human Factors and Ergonomics Society* (pp. 357–360). Santa Monica, CA: Human Factors and Ergonomics Society.

Endsley, M. R., & Kaber, D. B. (1999). Level of automation effects on performance, situation awareness and workload in dynamic control task. *Ergonomics, 42,* 462–492.

Endsley, M. R., & Robertson, M. M. (2000). Training for situation awareness. In M. R. Endsley & D. J. Garland (Eds.), *Situation awareness and measurement* (pp. 349–365). Mahwah, NJ: Lawrence Erlbaum Associates, Inc.

Fairclough, S. H., Venables, L., & Tattersall, A. (2005). The influence of task demand and learning on the psychophysiological response. *International Journal of Psychophysiology, 56,* 171–184.

Ferguson, G. A. (1981). *Statistical analysis in psychology and education* (5th ed.). Auckland, New Zealand: McGraw-Hill.

Garland, D. J., Wise, J. A., & Hopkin, V. D. (1999). *Handbook of aviation human factors.* Mahwah, NJ: Lawrence Erlbaum Associates, Inc.

Hansen, A. L., Johnsen, B. H., Sollers, J., Stenvik, K., & Thayer, J. (2004). Heart rate variability and its relation to prefrontal cognitive function: The effects of training and detraining. *European Journal of Applied Psychology, 93,* 263–272.

Hansen, A. L., Johnsen, B. H., & Thayer, J. F. (2003). Vagal influence on working memory and attention. *International Journal of Psychophysiology, 48,* 263–274.

Hayano, J., Sakakibara, Y., Yamada, A., Yamada, M., Mukai, T., Fujinami, T., et al. (1991). Accuracy of assessment of cardiac vagal tone by heart rate variability in normal subjects. *American Journal of Cardiology, 67,* 199–204.

Johnsen, B. H., Hansen, A. L., Sollers, J. J., Murison, R., & Thayer, J. F. (2002, March). *Heart rate variability is inversely related to cortisol reactivity during cognitive stress.* Paper presented at the annual meeting of the American Psychosomatic Society, Barcelona, Spain.

Johnsen, B. H., & Hugdahl, K. (1990). Fear questionnaires for simple phobias: Psychometric evaluations on a Norwegian sample. *Scandinavian Journal of Psychology, 31,* 42–48.

Jones, D. G. (2000). Subjective measures of situation awareness. In M. R. Endsley & D. J. Garland (Eds.), *Situation awareness and measurement* (pp. 113–128). Mahwah, NJ: Lawrence Erlbaum Associates, Inc.

Klaver, C. H. A. M., de Geus, E. J. C., & de Vries, J. (1994). Ambulatory monitoring system. In F. J. Maarse (Eds.), *Computers in psychology 5: Applications, methods and instrumentation* (pp. 254–268). Lisse, The Netherlands: Swets & Zeitlinger.

Klein, G. (2000). Analysis of situation awareness from critical incident reports. In M. R. Endsley & D. J. Garland (Eds.), *Situation awareness and measurement* (pp. 51–72). Mahwah, NJ: Lawrence Erlbaum Associates, Inc.

Magnusson, S. (2002). Similarities and differences in psychophysiological reactions between simulated and real air-to-ground missions. *International Journal of Aviation Psychology, 12,* 49–61.

Matthews, M. D., Beal, S. A., & Pleban, R. J. (2001). *Situation awareness in a virtual environment: Description of a subjective assessment scale* (Research Rep.). Alexandria, VA: U.S. Army Research Institute for the Behavioral and Social Sciences.

Matthews, M. D., Strater, L. D., & Endsley, M. R. (2004). Situation awareness requirements for infantry platoon leaders. *Military Psychology, 16,* 149–161.

Meshkati, N. (1988). Heart rate variability and mental workload assessment. In P. A. Hancock & N. Meshkati (Eds), *Human mental work load* (pp. 101–115). Amsterdam: Elsvier Science.

Orasanu, J., Dismukes, R. K., & Fischer, U. (1993). Decision errors in the cockpit. In *Proceedings of the Human Factors and Ergonomics Society 37th Annual Meeting* (pp. 363–367). Santa Monica, CA: Human Factors and Ergonomics Society.

Rodgers, M. D., Mogford, R. H., & Strauch, B. (2000). Post hoc assessment of situation awareness in air traffic control incidents and major aircraft accidents. In M. R. Endsley & D. J. Garland (Eds.), *Situation awareness and measurement* (pp. 73–112). Mahwah, NJ: Lawrence Erlbaum Associates, Inc.

Romano, D. M., & Brna, P. (2001). Presence and reflection in training: Support for learning to improve quality decision-making skills under time limitations. *Cyberpsychology & Behaviour, 4,* 265–277.

Salas, E., Prince, C., Baker, D. P., & Shrestha, L. (1995). Situation awareness in team performance: Implications for measurement and training. *Human Factors, 37,* 123–136.

Shebilske, W. L., Goettl, B. P., & Garland, D. J. (2000). Situation awareness, automaticity, and training. In M. R. Endsley & D. J. Garland (Eds.), *Situation awareness and measurement* (pp. 303–324). Mahwah, NJ: Lawrence Erlbaum Associates, Inc.

Shimamura, A. P. (2000). The role of the prefrontal cortex in dynamic filtering. *Psychophysiology, 28,* 207–218.

Svensson, E. A., AngelborgThanderz, M., Sjoberg, L., & Olsson, S. (1997). Information complexity— Mental workload and performance in combat aircraft. *Ergonomics, 40,* 362–380.

Svensson, E. A., & Wilson, G. F. (2002). Psychological and psychophysiological models of pilot performance for systems development and mission evaluation. *International Journal of Aviation Psychology, 12,* 95–110.

Thayer, J. F., Friedman, B. H., & Borkovec, T. D. (1996). Autonomic characteristics of general anxiety disorder and worry. *Biological Psychiatry, 39,* 255–266.

Thayer, J. F., & Lane, R. D. (2000). A model of neurovisceral integration in emotion regulation and dysregulation. *Journal of Affective Disorders, 61,* 201–216.

Vidulich, M. A., Stratton, M., Crabtree, M., & Wilson, G. (1994). Performance-based and physiological measures of situational awareness. *Aviation, Space, and Environmental Medicine, 65,* 7–12.

Waag, W. L., & Houck, M. R. (1994). Tools for assessing situational awareness in an operational fighter environment. *Aviation, Space, and Environmental Medicine, 65*(5, Suppl.), 13–19.

White, C. R., Carson, J. L., & Wilbourn, J. M. (1991a). Handgun marksmanship training: Evaluation of an advanced marksmanship trainer. *Performance Improvement Quarterly, 4,* 63–73.

White, C. R., Carson, J. L., & Wilbourn, J. M. (1991b). Training effectiveness of an M-16 rifle simulator. *Military Psychology, 3*, 177–184.

Wilcox, R. R. (1987). New designs in analysis of variance. *Annual Review Psychology, 38*, 29–60.

MILITARY PSYCHOLOGY, 2006, *18*(Suppl.). S23–S36

Shared Mental Models and Operational Effectiveness: Effects on Performance and Team Processes in Submarine Attack Teams

Roar Espevik
Department of Leadership Development
The Royal Norwegian Naval Academy
Bergen, Norway

Bjørn Helge Johnsen and Jarle Eid
Department of Psychosocial Science
University of Bergen, Norway
and the Royal Norwegian Navy

Julian F. Thayer
Department of Health Psychology
The Ohio State University

In this study submarine attack crews were studied during simulated attack operations. The aim of the study was to test whether knowledge about team members had an effect on performance and team processes. The design controlled for skills of the different operators. Briefly, this study demonstrated that knowledge about team members adds to performance, over and above the contribution from operational skills. This was evident for number of hits on target, amount of information exchange, and the type of information changed to a more controlling type of interaction when the attack teams operated. In addition, the data indicated less physiological arousal in teams with known team members. We attributed this effect to the shared mental models of team members when the attack teams operated under a condition of known team members.

Correspondence should be addressed to Roar Espevik, The Royal Norwegian Naval Academy, Pb 1 Haakonsvern, 5886 Bergen, Norway. E-mail: respevik@mil.no

In military organizations critical decisions are made every day by teams of individuals who must coordinate their activities to achieve optimal effectiveness. Decisions are often made under the strain of time pressure, uncertainty, and threat of fatal consequences. Complex high-tech systems and equipment have been introduced to facilitate meeting the challenges of command and control in operational environments. One consequence of this increasingly complex man–machine interface is the need to carefully coordinate and synchronize input from individual team members. Submarines constitute a specialized environment, characterized by careful selection and training of personnel, highly complex technology, and a unique organizational culture.

The ultimate challenge for a submarine crew is to function effectively when it must defend itself and attack enemy vessels. The submarine crew must be able to operate sophisticated equipment, integrate and exchange vital situational assessments, and execute actions against hostile contacts. Complex decisions must be made despite high workload, time pressure, uncertainty, and external threat. In addition salient stressors such as extremely limited work and living space, absence of day–night cues, confinement, isolation from all interactions with the external world, monotony in routine, and extended separation from family members constitute internal demands that submarine crews must master.

Research into team effectiveness has shown that effective teams can maintain performance even under conditions of high workload when communication opportunities are reduced (Kleiman & Serfaty, 1989). This has been labeled *implicit coordination* and depends on the teams' ability to draw on a common understanding of the task. Several authors have hypothesized that the mechanisms that allow this type of performance are shared mental models (SMMs; Cannon-Bowers, Salas, & Converse, 1993). Mental models involve mechanisms that humans use to describe the purpose and form of a system as well as its functioning in the present and future state (Rouse & Morris, 1986). Recently, researchers have emphasized the shared aspects of mental models in expert teams. SMMs are assumed to enable the team members to predict task needs and actions of other team members. SMM offers an understanding of how team members coordinate behavior and choose different actions without explicit demands to coordinate (Cannon-Bowers & Salas, 1998).

The significance of SMMs and team coordination was emphasized in the research project Tactical Decision Making Under Stress (TADMUS), initiated after the U.S.S. *Vincennes* shot down an Iranian Airbus in 1988. TADMUS is an applied research program in U.S. Department of Defense parlance. Briefly, the goal of the TADMUS program was to develop training, simulation, decision support, and display principles that would help mitigate the impact of stress on decision making (Cannon-Bowers & Salas, 1998). The program had a special emphasis on information processing and tactical decision making by shipboard command teams in air defense operations under conditions of short decision times, high operational workload, and ambiguous incomplete information. One of the conclusions from the TADMUS project was the importance of swift and accurate coordination of information and behavior to successfully cope with the demands of emergency combat situations. This implies the need for team coordination strategies that must be implicit and automatic (Kleinman & Serfaty, 1989). SMMs constitute a core aspect of a successful coordination of information and behavior in expert teams (Cannon-Bowers et al., 1993). Highly effective operational teams have multiple SMMs of different types and levels of complexity that enhance effective coordination and problem solving. Following the TADMUS project, a number of studies have indicated that SMM may contribute to increased team effectiveness (Volpe, Cannon-Bowers, Salas, & Spector, 1996).

Another significant outcome from the TADMUS project was its emphasis on naturalistic decision making (NDM) to study aspects of real-life decision making. NDM implies a focus on the individual decision maker and the decision process. Lipshitz and Ben Shaul (1996) stated that a common view in the different NDM models is the focus on recognition of situations and reflection processes as a continuous shift between thought and action. The actual situation at hand is compared to similar situations, actions, and outcomes. The decision maker focuses not on a particular problem, but uses his or her experience with similar situations to implement different solutions to a series of problems. The dominating model in NDM is recognition primed decision making (RPD; Klein, 1998). In RPD an expert decision maker is believed to make use of previous experience and expertise to detect familiar elements and information patterns that can be used to assess the situation and solve the problem at hand.

The TADMUS project also focused on team performance. Team output gives a good indication of team efficiency. However, team performance is also related to information sharing, implicit and explicit coordination, and team-member exchange to solve operational tasks. In other words, team performance hinges on several underlying processes occurring in the team during task executing. The TADMUS project identified supporting behavior, team initiative, information exchange, and communication as significant aspects of team performance (Smith-Jentsch, Zeisig, Acton, & McPherson, 1998).

Research in the TADMUS project was largely performed on teams operating on antiair warfare in U.S. Navy vessels (Combat Information Centre Anti-Air Warfare teams [CiC team]). The environments these teams must master are characterized by dependence of team effort, proficiency of specific and shared tasks, and distinct roles among the team members (see Duncan et al., 1996, for an overview). Through in-depth interviews, observations, and comparison of errors between experts and novices in expert teams, a number of core characteristics of SMMs were extracted. These characteristics of the high-performing, high-SMM teams were summarized in six hypotheses. First, the team members will be more accurate in predicting the actions of their teammates. Second, team members will require less overt planning time to accomplish their mission. Third, teams will spend less time communicating. Fourth, the frequency of requests to repeat information or ask why a team member is taking some action will be reduced. Fifth, activities will be better sequenced, without discussion, because team members will know what and when to communicate to whom. Finally, teams will be more resilient to stress effects. Although stressors normally reduce the amount of information flow through the CiC, thereby limiting the tasks they can perform, an SMM will allow them to coordinate implicitly using an internal model of the team (Duncan et al., 1996, p. 185).

Orasanu (1990, cited in Stout, Cannon-Bowers, Salas, & Milanovich, 1999) showed that effective aircrews met difficult situations with an increased amount of unasked information. At the same time the captains reduced requests for information. Less effective teams showed the opposite information exchange strategies. In the TADMUS project, the information exchange strategies used by effective teams were interpreted as an index of the presence of an SMM in the team. It was stated that an SMM made it possible for the team to give each other vital information in a proper and orderly manner without the receiver asking for it. This enabled the team to focus on the essentials in the task they were facing. Thus the number of times unsolicited information was offered was seen as a vital confirmation of the presence of an SMM (Duncan et al., 1996).

An SMM is based on the assumption that the team must be able to simulate future events to create good and plausible explanations of future outcomes. To make this possible, some researchers have suggested that multiple shared models must be in action at the same time. Rouse and Morris (1986) suggested a taxonomy of mental models where every level or type of model has different importance depending on which task one wants to solve. Some problems are solved through one type of mental model, and other problems are solved by integrating several mental models.

The TADMUS study identified four levels or types of SMM: (a) the equipment, (b) task at hand, (c) team interaction, and (d) type of team (Cannon-Bowers et al., 1993). The SMMs related to the equipment, task, and team interaction are particularly emphasized in the TADMUS project. Some empirical studies have focused on the importance of knowledge about tasks, need of information, and the entire team (Duncan et al., 1996). The fourth type of SMM is related to knowledge about individual differences in competencies, skills, abilities, preferences, and tendencies (Cannon-Bowers et al., 1993). In spite of repeated statements of the importance of SMM of team members, few if any empirical studies of this factor have been published.

Thus, it is still an open issue if the SMM of the team influences team performance and resilience toward stress. This could lead to a hypothesis that both knowledge about how to act and knowledge about individual team members will influence team performance and effectiveness. One way to explore the effect of an SMM of team members would be to study seasoned and well-established military teams, such as submarine attack crews. These teams are relatively small, well trained, and have a high degree of both operational skill and personal knowledge. To study team performance in a realistic and true-to-life operational setting, a full-scale submarine simulator provides several advantages. First, these simulators are exact copies of operational submarines. Second, simulators offer several options for monitoring performance and tracking individual performance over time.

The aim of this study was to investigate whether knowledge about individual team members would augment the effect of operational skills in predicting operational effectiveness in trained expert teams. More specifically, would an SMM of team members add to the performance of the team, over and above that explained by operational skills? We hypothesized that known team members—those familiar with one another—would show better performance and less cardiovascular reactivity to a simulated tactical situation compared to unknown team members.

METHOD

Participants

The total population of attack teams on the Norwegian ULA class submarines participated in the study. Twenty-four active duty officers composed four attack teams (six members per team). The officers were ranked from lieutenant commander to sublieutenant. The purpose of the attack team was to discover, classify, and eventually attack when operating against an imaginary or real enemy.

The participants' mean age was 26.3 years (range = 24–33) and experience ranged from 4 to 12 years. All members of the attack teams had worked together as teams for more than 3 months.

Outcome Variables

Interpositional knowledge. A questionnaire was developed to evaluate operational knowledge in the teams. The questionnaire was based on *interpositional knowledge* (IPK; Volpe et al., 1996). This IPK was developed in cooperation with expert personnel in the submarine service. IPK refers to the amount of knowledge a team member has of others, their own, and the team's tasks, roles and proper responses in different situations. The IPK was divided into two parts. Part 1 deals with the member's knowledge about different positions in the attack teams, their roles, tasks, responsibilities, and duties. Part 2 concerns knowledge about the system and what to do given different situations or system status. The IPK consisted of 17 items. Here is an example of an item: "The submarine has 8 torpedoes on the way. Sonar reports comprimated cavitation. What can and should each position in the attack team contribute in this situation?" The items were scored by expert raters and given scores from 1 to 3 based on the quality of their answers. Each person and subsequently each attack team was given a total score.

Performance variables.   The attack teams and their reactions were observed during two different war games in a ULA-class tactical trainer. This simulator is a replica of the submarine central, the natural work space of an attack team. The simulator presented information about own speed and depth as well as all information available about other ships that would be present for the attack team on board a real ULA-class submarine. Computer software in the simulator recorded target solutions, firing range, hits, and course and speed of own and other vessels. Criteria-based evaluation of efficiency consisted of accuracy, latency, and mission effectiveness (Cannon-Bowers & Salas, 1998). Latency was measured as distance in meters to targets at the moment of firing and when it was actually hit. Mission effectiveness was the number of torpedoes hitting the target.

Process variables.   Teamwork was evaluated on four dimensions: information exchange, communication, supporting behavior, and team initiative (based on ATOM; Smith-Jentsch et al., 1998).

Verbal processes were examined using video and audio tape recordings (Sony TCM-459V) and video (Sony Super Steady Shot Handycam video HI8 CCD TR2200E PAL; Serfaty, Entin, & Johnston, 1998). The number of statements was registered as total amount (statements per minute) and separated into three categories: request, transfer, and confirmation. Request and transfer were divided into information, actions, and problem solving (see Serfaty et al., 1998). In addition, statements confirming request and transfer were registered. Every statement was also registered with respect to the sender and the receiver.

Psychophysiological arousal.   Cardiovascular responses were measured by using the Ambulatory Monitoring System V. 3. 6. (AMS; Klaver, de Geus, & de Vries, 1994). The cardiac responses were measured with 8 mm Ag/AgCl ECG electrodes (Cleartrode, Disposable Pregelled Electrodes, 150, Standard Silver). One electrode was placed over the jugular notch of the sternum, between the collarbones; another was placed 4 cm under the left ribs; and the third electrode was placed at the right lateral side between the two lower ribs. Heart rate was recorded as beats per minute (bpm).

Procedure

The study was conducted in the tactical submarine simulator for the ULA-class submarine situated at Haakonsvern Naval Base in Bergen, Norway. Norwegian submarine crews use the tactical simulator as part of their normal enhancement training. The training program follows established demands and progression levels. All four attack teams were experienced users of the simulator at the time of this study. The head of submarine simulator training noted that the teams were equivalent in terms of performance. All four attack teams were rated as operational and approved by their superiors to be functioning on the highest level within 2 months prior to this study.

The two war game scenarios used in this study were consistent with the training program the attack teams normally go through and identical for all teams. The scenarios were event based (Johnston, Payne, & Smith-Jentsch, 1998), following the same design used in the studies of the TADMUS project. The war games were comprised of realistic stressors that gave the teams an increasing amount of workload and need for coordination. Three experienced submarine experts evaluated both war games as realistic and consisting of the necessary stress level.

The participants completed the IPK questionnaire and were then equipped with the AMS before entering the simulator. Ten minutes before each war game started, the commanding officer got a description of the situation his team was supposed to handle. Each of the two war games lasted 50 min. One game was run with an intact original team (known team). The second run was performed with a second in command (2iC) from a different team (unknown team). The runs were administered in balanced order.

To look at stress reactivity, each run was separated into two distinct phases. The low-stress phase involved classification and calculations of bearings of opponents. The last 10 min (high-stress phase) involved a high-stress situation in which the attack teams had several torpedoes in the water and a manipulated problem with the torpedoes. The problem was identical for all teams and both conditions. In addition, the submarine was attacked by a hostile submarine.

Statistical Analyses

T tests for independent samples were used to test differences in IPK between the different attack teams. Analyses of performance during the simulator run were based on a repeated measures design (Ferguson, 1981), and t tests for dependent samples were used to test differences between the two conditions. Due to the specific predictions about the directions of the means, one-tailed tests were used (Ferguson, 1981). Analyses of physiological arousal were performed using a 2 (known vs. unknown teams) × 2 (low-stress vs. high-stress phase) factorial design (Ferguson, 1981), using a two-way analysis of variance (ANOVA); both factors were treated as repeated measures. Preplanned simple effects and contrasts were performed by means of one-tailed t tests due to the clear predictions of the direction of the means (Wilcox, 1987).

RESULTS

Preconditions

No differences between the teams on IPK were found. Examination of the scores on the IPK of the four 2iC teams indicated that the four scores were almost identical.

Performance

Better performance measured as number of hits on target was found for known teams compared to unknown teams, $t(3) = 2.45$, $p < .05$. This can be seen in Figure 1, where known teams shows better performance than unknown teams.

The criteria-based measurement of performance also showed a nonsignificant tendency toward superior behavior of known teams. Although not significant, there was a trend for known teams to discover, classify, attack, and hit targets at a longer distance than unknown teams. Known teams fired their weapons at a mean distance of 59,657 m compared to a distance of 55,200 m for unknown teams. Known teams also hit their targets from longer distance ($M = 30,325$ m) compared to unknown teams ($M = 21,625$ m).

Team Processes

Rate of information exchange was significantly different between the two groups (see Figure 2). A higher volume of verbal statements occurred in the unknown team member group compared to the known group, $t(23) = 1.78$, $p < .05$.

When looking at types of information exchange, unknown teams showed higher frequencies of requests, $t(23) = 1.81$, $p < .05$. These requests were separated

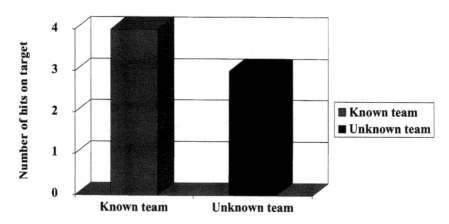

FIGURE 1   Mean number of hits on target for the unknown and the known team.

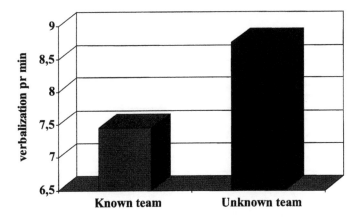

FIGURE 2   Mean number of verbalizations per minute.

into request for information, request for action, and request for solving a problem. Unknown teams showed higher frequencies on all these measures: $t(3) = 2.24$, $p < .05$; $t(3) = 3.36$, $p < .05$; and $t(3) = 2.35$, $p < .05$, respectively (see Figure 3).

An indication of a similar pattern was discovered for the analyses of transfer of information, transfer of action, and transfer of problem solving. There was a trend toward higher level of information transfer in the unknown group compared to the known group, $t(3) = 1.84$, $p < .08$ (one-tailed). There were also nonsignificant tendencies toward higher numbers of transfer of actions and problem solving for the unknown compared to the known teams.

When investigating which position contributed most to the increase in information exchange between the two conditions, a clear picture emerged. The command-

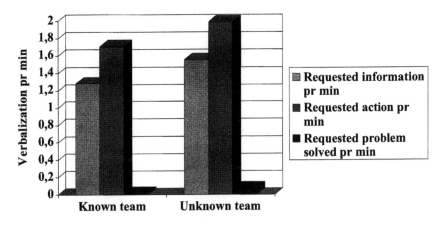

FIGURE 3   Mean number of verbalizations per minute in three information categories.

TABLE 1
Quantity of Information Exchange Separated for Different Positions
in the Attack Team

Information Exchange Commanding Officer–Crew–2iC	Known 2iC		Unknown 2iC	
	M	SD	M	SD
Commanding officer–crew	2.90	0.47	3.25	0.82
Crew–commanding officer	2.30	0.41	2.63	1.03
Commanding officer–2iC*	1.12	0.75	1.63	0.65
2iC–commanding officer	1.04	0.60	1.52	0.61

Note.   2iC = second in command.
*p < .05.

ing officer verbalized significantly more to the unknown 2iC, $t(3) = 2.67, p < .05$, and the unknown 2iC's verbalization to the commanding officer tended to be higher compared to that of the known 2iC, $t(3) = 2.02, p < .07$. As can be seen in Table 1, all exchange of information in the triad—commanding officer, the rest of the crew, 2iC—increased when the 2iC was unknown.

When positional information exchange was paired with type of information it showed that the commanding officer had significantly more requests to his unknown 2iC, $t(3) = 5.8, p < .05$, compared to the known 2iC. Unknown 2iCs made significantly more requests to the commanding officer compared to known 2iCs, $t(3) = 3.45, p < .05$. The categories of transfer and confirmation were significantly higher from unknown 2iC to commanding officer compared to known 2iC, $t(3) = 2.29, p < .05$, and $t(3) = 1.68 , p < .05$ (one-tailed), respectively. No other significant effects were found.

Psychophysiological Arousal

Analyses of cardiovascular activity showed a borderline significant main effect of groups, $F(1, 22) = 3.62, p < .07$, with higher heart rate (HR) during the unknown team condition. Furthermore, a borderline main effect was found for the high-stress compared to the low-stress phase, resulting in higher HR in the high-stress phase, $F(1, 22) = 3.4, p < .07$.

Preplanned contrasts showed that the only significant difference found was an increase in HR from low-stress to high-stress phase in unknown teams ($p < .05$; see Figure 4).

DISCUSSION

This study showed superior performance in known submarine attack teams compared to unknown teams. When expert teams changed from an unknown 2iC to a

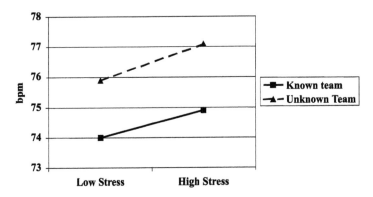

FIGURE 4   Heart rate (beats per minute) for known and unknown teams, in high-stress and low-stress phases.

well-known 2iC, the number of torpedoes on target increased, information exchange decreased, and members showed less physiological stress reaction.

The main purpose of a submarine attack team is to sink enemy ships with torpedoes. This study showed that attack teams composed of well-known team members had more hits by torpedoes compared to teams with an unknown 2iC. This was found although the teams and the officers had equal knowledge and experience about the system they operated. It could be argued that teams with a well-known 2iC had an SMM that facilitated performance.

This expands previous knowledge about SMMs, where the focus has been on equipment, task, and team interaction (Cannon-Bowers et al., 1993). Performance data were further supported by a pattern of nonsignificant results that all pointed in the same direction. This was the case, for example, with the variable of distance to target when firing and correct classifications. Thus, disrupting the SMM of expert members, while keeping the level of knowledge of equipment, tasks, and roles constant, decreased performance on crucial aspects of the submarine's performance.

The analyses of team processes showed that the amount of information was higher in the unknown group. It has been assumed that well-developed SMMs enable teams to coordinate their activities in a way that increases their ability to cope with external threats (Kleinman & Serfaty, 1989). Through SMMs, team members have better capability to predict other team members' actions and need for information (Cannon-Bowers et al., 1993). Thus, the need for explicit coordination of information transfer will be lower in teams with a highly developed SMM (Kleinman & Serfaty, 1989). In this study, it could be argued that the increased exchange of information seen in the unknown team was an indication of a lack of an SMM of the team members. This argument could be valid because all teams had similar operational SMMs (equipment, task, and roles).

The significance of an SMM of team members also became evident in the analyses of types of information exchanged. In this study, the types of information were categorized in two major categories: requests and transfers. These categories were further divided into information (need to know), actions (demanding the execution of an order), and solving a problem (need something to be done; Serfaty et al., 1998). The results of this study showed higher levels of all measures of request and a borderline difference in transfer. The unknown attack teams exchanged information to a greater degree and the information was more controlling. This was a change in coordination strategy from a more implicit strategy in the known attack teams, to an explicit controlling strategy when the teams changed from a well-known 2iC to an unknown 2iC. The substance of the statements used in the explicit strategy was dominated by a need for increased control over the team members. Significantly more requests and transfers give a clear indication that unknown teams needed to coordinate their activity verbally through checking that something was done in a proper manner. This shows that teams without an SMM of the team members coordinate their activity differently and less efficiently than those with such an SMM. This is in line with Urban, Bowers, Monday, and Morgan (1995), who claimed in a study of hierarchical and nonhierarchical teams that efficient teams are characterized by minimized use of question–answer sequences. Our study also showed that teams with an SMM of the team members showed reduced question–answer sequences.

Further analyses of the information exchange within the attack teams revealed an interesting pattern. This pattern showed that more information was exchanged between the commanding officer and the 2iC in the unknown teams. There was also more information exchange from the 2iC to the commanding officer in the unknown teams. This gives further support to the notion that the information structure in the unknown team was distorted, and it was characterized by the need for the commanding officer and the 2iC to coordinate and control each orders needs, intentions, and actions. The commanding officer and the 2iC were the team members that made most of the decisions. Thus, the lack of an SMM among team members results in an increase in the need for explicit coordination among the team's senior decision makers.

One aspect of the TADMUS project was the extensive use of randomly composed teams of experts (Duncan et al., 1996). Expert teams are not just an aggregate of highly skilled operators working together. It could be argued that an expert team also consists of members with extensive knowledge about each team member and that they have trained and served together over a prolonged period of time. This study supports the importance of this notion and shows that not only will expert teams with an SMM of the team members show improved performance, but also show increased stress resilience. This is based on the findings that only the unknown teams showed a significant increase in HR from low-intensity to high-intensity scenarios. HR is often used as a measure of a stress response (Kudielka,

Buske-Kirschbaum, Hellhammer, & Kirschbaum, 2004) and Schommer, Hellhammer, and Kirschbaum (2004) showed a decrease in HR during the stress response over time. As can be seen from this study, the groups without an SMM of the team members showed an increase in HR over time as the workload increased, but only when they were exposed to a condition with an unknown 2iC.

The research described in the TADMUS project was based on studies performed on participants recruited from the U.S. Navy or U.S. colleges (Cannon-Bowers & Salas, 1998). Although there are cultural differences between the U.S. Navy and the Norwegian Navy, the theoretical framework of SMMs appears quite applicable to teamwork in the Norwegian Navy.

In summary, this study demonstrated that knowledge about team members (i.e., SMM of the team members) adds to performance over and above the contribution of operational skills. This was evident for performance evaluations like number of hits on target, as well as team processes like information exchange. The need for controlling types of information was higher when teams changed from a known 2iC to an unknown 2iC. Stress reactivity, measured by HR, increased from a low-stress to a high-stress situation only in the teams without a highly developed SMM of the team members. This study has implications for training and rotation of personnel in expert teams. Mastery of rules, procedures, and skills is not enough for high performance in a crew. Personnel need to develop an SMM of the other team members. Keeping crews intact during training and operations could do this. Rotation of personnel among different vessels and expert teams may result in decreased efficiency. Although the effects of known team members add to the performance of knowledge in expert teams, well-known teams could be more negatively affected by negative group processes like groupthink and other socially induced biases (Janis, 1972).

In addition, a need for further studies on the effects of SMMs of team members is called for. This is especially true because there is an increased emphasis on networkcentric warfare, where different expert teams must coordinate their activities. These teams are often located apart and SMMs of team members could influence the performance of these teams.

REFERENCES

Cannon-Bowers, J. A., & Salas, E. (1998). *Making decisions under stress*. Washington, DC: American Psychological Association.

Cannon-Bowers, J. A., Salas, E., & Converse, S. (1993). Shared mental models. In J. N. Castellan (Ed.), *Individual and group decision making* (pp. 221–246). Hillsdale, NJ: Lawrence Erlbaum Associates, Inc.

Duncan, P. C., Rouse, W. B., Johnston, J. H., Cannon-Bowers, J. A., Salas, E., & Burns, J. (1996). Training teams working in complex systems: A mental model approach. In W. E. Rouse (Ed.), *Human/technology interaction in complex systems* (pp. 173–233). Greenwich, CT: JAI Press.

Ferguson, G. A. (1981). *Statistical analysis in psychology and education.* New York: McGraw-Hill.
Janis, I. L. (1972). *Group think: Psychological studies of policy fiascoes* (2nd ed.). Boston: Houghton-Mifflin.
Johnston, J. H., Payne, S. C., & Smith-Jentsch, K. A. (1998). Measuring team-related expertise in complex environments. In J. A. Cannon-Bowers & E. Salas (Eds.), *Making decisions under stress* (pp. 61–88). Washington, DC: American Psychological Association.
Klaver, G. H. A. M., de Geus, E. J. H., & de Vries, J. (1994). Ambulatory monitoring system. In I. F. J. Maarse (Ed.), *Computers in psychology 5: Application methods and instrumentation* (pp. 254–268). Lisse, The Netherlands: Swets & Zeitlinger.
Klein, G. (1998). *Sources of power: How people make decisions.* Cambridge, MA: MIT Press.
Kleinman, D. L., & Serfaty, D. (1989). Team performance assessment in distributed decision making. In R. Gilson, J. P. Kincaid, & B. Goldiez (Eds.), *Proceedings: Interactive network simulation for training conference* (pp. 22–27). Orlando, FL: Naval Training System Center.
Kudielka, B. M., Buske-Kirschbaum, A., Hellhammer, D. H., & Kirschbaum, C. (2004). Differential heart rate reactivity and recovery after psychosocial stress (TSST) in healthy children, younger adults, and elderly adults: The impact of age and gender. *International Journal of Behavioral Medicine, 11*, 116–121.
Lipshitz, R., & Ben Shaul, O. (1996). Schemata and mental models in recognition-primed decision making. In G. Klein & C. Zsambok (Eds.), *Naturalistic decision making* (pp. 293–304). Hillsdale, NJ: Lawrence Erlbaum Associates, Inc.
Rouse, W. B., & Morris, N. M. (1986). On looking into the black box: Prospects and limits in the search for mental models. *Psychological Bulletin, 100*, 349–363.
Schommer, N. C., Hellhammer, D. H., & Kirschbaum, C. (2004). Dissociation between reactivity of the hypothalamus-pituitary-adrenal axis and the sympathetic-adrenal-medullary system to repeated psychosocial stress. *Psychosomatic Medicine, 65*, 450–460.
Serfaty, D., Entin, E. E., & Johnston, J. H. (1998). *Team coordination training.* In J. A. Cannon-Bowers & E. Salas (Eds.), *Making decisions under stress* (pp. 221–245). Washington, DC: American Psychological Association.
Smith-Jentsch, K. A., Zeisig, R. L., Acton, B., & McPherson, J. A. (1998). Team dimensional training: A strategy for guided team self-correction. In J. A. Cannon-Bowers & E. Salas (Eds.), *Making decisions under stress* (pp. 271–297). Washington, DC: American Psychological Association.
Stout, R. J., Cannon-Bowers, J. A., Salas, E., & Milanovich, D. M. (1999). Planning, shared mental models, and coordinated performance: An empirical link is established. *Human Factors, 41*, 61–71.
Urban, J. M., Bowers, C. A., Monday, S. D., & Morgan, B. B. (1995). Workload, team structure, and communication in team performance. *Military Psychology, 7*, 123–139.
Volpe, C. E., Cannon-Bowers, J. A., Salas, E., & Spector, P. E. (1996). The impact of cross-training on team functioning: An empirical investigation. *Human Factors, 38*, 87–100.
Wilcox, R. R. (1987). New design in analysis of variance. *Annual Review of Psychology, 38*, 29–60.

MILITARY PSYCHOLOGY, 2006, *18*(Suppl.), S37–S56

EDUCATION

Moral Behavior and Transformational Leadership in Norwegian Naval Cadets

Olav Kjellevold Olsen
Department of Leader Development
The Royal Norwegian Naval Academy
Bergen, Norway

Jarle Eid and Bjørn Helge Johnsen
Department of Psychosocial Science
University of Bergen, Norway
and the Royal Norwegian Navy

This study explores the relation between indicators of moral behavior and peer ratings of leadership behavior in Norwegian naval officer cadets ($N = 172$). Moral reasoning (Rest, Narvaez, Bebeau, & Thoma, 1999b) and moral identity (Aquino & Reed, 2002) were used as predictor variables, and peer rating of leadership behavior (Bass & Avolio, 1995) was used as the primary outcome measure. The results indicated that postconventional moral reasoning and moral identity were positively correlated with transactional and transformational leadership behavior, and they were negatively correlated with passive–avoidant leadership behavior. A stepwise hierarchical regression analysis revealed that indicators of moral behavior explained 10% to 14% of the variance in passive–avoidant, transactional, and transformational leader behavior. Furthermore, indicators of moral behavior emerged as significant predictor variables for the transformational facets of idealized influence (17%), inspirational motivation (12%), and individualized consideration (16%). Finally, indicators of moral behavior also predicted the transactional facet of contingent reward (11%), the passive–avoidant facets of management-by-exception–passive (8%), and laissez-faire (9%). Taken together these data indicate that individual differences in

Correspondence should be addressed to Olav Kjellevold Olsen, The Royal Norwegian Naval Academy, P.O. Box 83 Haakonsvern, 5886 Bergen, Norway. E-mail: olavolsen@mil.no

moral reasoning and moral identity significantly affect leadership behavior, and may have implications for training and selection of military personnel.

Military doctrines (Department of the Army, 2004; U.S. Marine Corps, 1997) and recent experience from operations like those in Iraq and Afghanistan (Bartone, 2004; Taguba, 2004) have emphasized the significance of leadership and ethics as preconditions to operational success. Despite an enduring focus on ethics in the military, surprisingly few empirical studies have addressed the relation between moral behavior and leadership behavior in a military setting. Thus the main focus of this study was to explore whether indicators of moral behavior (i.e., moral reasoning and the self-importance of moral identity) might be associated with leadership behavior in a sample of Norwegian naval cadets.

IS THERE A MORAL COMPONENT IN TRANSFORMATIONAL LEADERSHIP?

The relation between morals and leadership has been a long-standing issue in leadership theory. On the one hand some theoretical perspectives have stated that successful leaders must be able to manipulate, deceive, and take advantage of their subordinates (and opponents) to achieve leadership success (Bailey, 1988). On the other hand more recent theories have emphasized ethics and morals at the heart of successful leadership (Burns, 1978; Ciulla, 1998; Gardner, 1990). Burns (1978) described the *transformational leader* as a morally mature agent who focuses on developing the moral maturity, values, and ideals of his or her subordinates and strengthening their commitment to serve the well-being of others, their organization, and society beyond self-interest. This differs from the *transactional leader,* who emphasizes control over subordinates by the use of corrective transactions (contingency theory) aimed at fulfilling the personal needs of the subordinates in exchange for a specific work effort.

An accumulated body of research has shown that transformational leadership has a strong impact on desirable outcomes such as organizational efficiency, job satisfaction, and organizational commitment in civilian (Bass, 1998b; Lowe, Kroeck, & Sivasubrahmaniam, 1996), as well as in military organizations (Bass, Avolio, Jung, & Beson, 2003; Eid et al., 2004). Still, the ethical component of transformational leadership has been questioned (Bass & Steidlmeier, 1999). For example, Conger and Kanungo (1988) pointed out that highly charismatic and self-serving transformational leaders might exploit and deceive their subordinates. In the same vein, immoral transformational leaders might persuade subordinates to engage in immoral and evil activities (Stevens, D'Intio, & Victor, 1995).

BASS ON THE MORAL COMPONENT
IN TRANSFORMATIONAL LEADERSHIP

When Bass (1985) initially operationalized Burns's theory on transformational leadership it represented a shift from a morally based leadership theory into a morally neutral orientation (Ciulla, 1998). Consistent with Weber (1924/1947), Bass (1985) claimed that effective leaders could be either immoral or moral, deemphasizing the importance of moral competency in leadership (Bass & Steidlmeier, 1999). In the full range of leadership model, Bass (1998b) divided transformational leadership into four components: (a) idealized influence (by inspiring visions, sharing risks and hardships, and earning trust and confidence from their subordinates), (b) inspirational motivation (display enthusiasm and optimism in ways that motivate those around them by providing meaning and challenges), (c) intellectual stimulation (stimulating efforts to find new ideas and creative solutions to existing problems, encouraging innovation, creativity, and new approaches), and (d) individualized consideration (recognizing that subordinates have different needs and desires, and acting as a coach to develop their full potential).

Bass (1985) further divided transactional leadership into three components: (a) contingent reward (providing rewards contingent on performance), (b) management-by-exception–active (monitoring behavior and correcting anticipated errors), and (c) management-by-exception–passive (responding to errors and correcting problems if they have occurred). In addition to the transformational and transactional behaviors, Bass originally also included a laissez-faire style as a distinct form of dysfunctional leadership behavior. Later research has suggested that the management by exception–passive dimension should be combined with laissez-faire leadership to form a new dimension called passive–avoidant leadership (Avolio, Bass, & Jung, 1999; Bass & Avolio, 2000; Den Hartog, Van Muijen, & Koopman, 1997). Based on a principal component analysis, Hetland and Sandal (2003) found that the factors of contingent reward and management-by-exception–active could be defined as a coherent transactional factor in a Norwegian setting of business managers. In his full range leadership model, Bass stated that to be effective, leaders must master all components, but employ the transformational components most frequently, which substantially augments the effects of transactional leadership (Waldman, Bass, & Yammarino, 1990).

In recent work, Bass (1998a, 1998b; Bass & Steidlmeier, 1999) explicitly advocates moral character and ethical behavior as both a precondition for and an outcome of transformational leadership. By claiming that moral competency is vital to transformational leadership, Bass and coworkers seem to have closed the gap toward Burns's initial theory (Ciulla, 1998). However, the issue still remains about how to operationalize this moral competency.

Bass addressed the moral issue by introducing the concept of authentic transformational leaders who are genuinely committed to serving their peers, organization, or community (Bass, 1998a, 1998b). In contrast, the pseudo-transformational leaders would exhibit many transformational characteristics, but in the long run only cater to personal self-interest. This dichotomy has been criticized for not taking into account cognitive processes, and for underestimating the complexity of moral psychology (Price, 2003). It has therefore been suggested that research on morals and leadership behavior should include a variety of moral developmental constructs, such as moral sensitivity, moral motivation, and moral character (Rest, 1986; Turner, Barling, Epitropaki, Butcher, & Milner, 2002). In this study, we therefore used a multivariable approach to index moral behavior, including a measure of domination of moral schemas (Rest, Narvaez, Bebeau, & Thoma, 1999a) and self-importance of moral identity as a social-psychological motivator to moral conduct (Aquino & Reed, 2002).

TRANSFORMATIONAL LEADERSHIP THEORY AND MORAL REASONING

Kohlberg (1984) suggested in his cognitive theory on moral development that people organize their moral reasoning within six different concepts of justice. Along the same lines, Rest, Narvaez, Bebeau, and Thoma (1999a, 1999b) suggested that people make sense of moral situations in terms of three developmental moral schemas. These cognitive schemas structure and guide moral thinking in qualitatively different ways. The personal-interest schema represents the most premature schema, where moral thinking is instrumentally oriented toward fulfilling egocentric ends. The maintaining-norms schema represents the next developmental stage, where thinking is structured by a need to maintain a system of rules and regulations to secure stability and cooperative exchange in an often hostile and unpredictable world. The postconventional schema represents the most advanced stage in emphasizing that moral obligations must be based on universal moral principles like justice, fairness, and equality, which are open to public scrutiny and debate. At this stage the individual moral obligations serve higher purpose goals and ideals, which again might facilitate commitment and loyalty from peers and subordinates (Rawles, 1971).

From previous research one may deduce several reasons why officers with a high score on the postconventional schema would be more likely to use transformational behavior, and why officers high on the maintaining-norms schema would be seen as more transactional leaders. In line with Bass's (1998a, 1998b) definition of authentic transformational leadership, we would expect that leaders high on postconventional thinking would be more likely to value goals that serve the common good, even at the expense of immediate self-interests and instrumentalism. We would also expect a connection between the maintaining-norms schema and a preference for transactional leadership focusing on agreements and exchange of rewards and corrections to achieve effective cooperation (Bass, 1998a, 1998b). Second, we expect that leaders dominated by the postconventional schema are more able to manage or to balance the interests of various stakeholders (including minorities) in the organization through just and impartial distribution of rights and duties (Rawles, 1971; Rest et al., 1999a, 1999b). In this way, a postconventional moral schema might foster mutual trust and commitment toward a common good. The transformational facets of idealized influence (from leader behavior that instills respect and admiration) and the facet of inspirational motivation that provides subordinates with meaning in pursuing shared goals may be particularly important in this respect.

In addition to this, previous research has also indicated that the postconventional moral schema predicts moral behavior (Blasi, 1980; King & Mayhew, 2002; Rest, 1986). This moral behavior may facilitate trust in and respect for the leader, which is consistent with the effects of idealized influence, where subordinates strive to identify with and emulate the leader (Bass, 1998a, 1998b; Popper & Mayseless, 2003).

Finally, we expect that leaders dominated by the postconventional moral schema encourage a moral discourse and an open debate on moral issues in the organization that again may raise the independent moral conscience and level of moral reasoning of the subordinates (Burns, 1978; Dukerich, Nichols, Elm, & Vollrath, 1990). We expect that this pattern might load on both intellectual stimulation and individual consideration. Taken together this leads to our first working hypothesis:

H1: Scores on the postconventional schema are positively related to peer ratings of transformational leadership, and scores on the maintaining-norms and personal-interest schema are negatively associated with transformational leadership.

Turner et al. (2002) established some support for this hypothesis in a study of 130 Canadian and British middle-level managers. They recommended a replication of the study to test for sample biases. We further expected that the maintaining-norms schema would be linked to transactional leadership behavior, and characteristic of officers who define their leadership in terms of exchange and reciprocity.

H2: Scores on the maintaining-norms schema are positively related to peer ratings of transactional leadership.

Kuhnert and Lewis (1987) suggested that developmental theory, which focuses on changes and growth in leaders' perspective-taking abilities, explains changes in their way of construing reality and leadership behaviors. In this study we suggest that passive–avoidant leadership behavior (laissez-faire and management-by-exception–passive) might be explained by underdeveloped perspective-taking abilities (self-orientated) indicated by low scores on the postconventional moral schema and high scores on the personal-interest schema, which hinders leaders in perceiving the social context accurately and focusing on coworkers and the organization as a whole (Rawles, 1971). This cognitive shortcoming may be perceived as neglecting leadership responsibilities, consistent with passive–avoidant leadership.

> H3: Scores on the personal-interest schema are positively related to peer rat
> ings of passive–avoidant leadership behavior, and scores on the postcon
> ventional moral schema are negatively associated with passive–avoidant
> leadership behavior.

TRANSFORMATIONAL LEADERSHIP THEORY
AND THE SELF-IMPORTANCE OF MORAL IDENTITY

Although principled moral reasoning is believed to be an important factor, it only partially explains moral behavior (Blasi, 1980; Rest, 1986). Transformational leaders should also master a variety of moral competencies to be able to meet moral challenges (Turner et al., 2002). Rest (1986) introduced the *moral motivation* construct, defined as primacy of moral values (if in conflict with nonmoral values), as an important intervening variable to transform judgment into moral behavior. Along the same lines Gibbs (2004) identified a strong moral self-awareness as a common trait in morals-centered individuals, indicating that people who see morality as a central part of their own identity are more likely to be motivated to act morally.

According to Aquino and Reed (2002) moral identity could be seen as a social identity that forms a basis for social identification and self-definition. They argued that moral identity, if important to the individual, is an independent factor that will augment moral reasoning in producing moral behavior through self-regulatory mechanisms (Blasi, 1984). This implies that people with a strong moral identity would strive to maintain consistency between conceptions of their moral self and their actions in the world. In defining moral identity Aquino and Reed (2002) identified two distinct dimensions of the moral self: internalized moral identity (the private and personal arena) and symbolized moral identity (the public arena).

In this study we anticipated that a strong moral identity (highly important to the self-concept) would have a positive correlation with transformational behavior, and a negative correlation with passive–avoidant behavior. Following Aquino and Reed (2002) we also expected that moral identity would augment the effect of moral reasoning in predicting transformational leadership and passive–avoidant leadership. Leaders who stand out as positive examples will be admired and respected by their subordinates, which is in line with the transformational component of idealized influence. Furthermore, leaders who are more oriented toward the moral aspects of the leader–subordinate exchange might also sensitize their subordinates to moral concerns and facilitate a working environment characterized by consideration for the individual, which again may influence subordinates to focus their attention toward the same issues (Aquino & Reed, 2002). This may facilitate a more sensitive and reflective work environment, which might be stimulated by the transformational components of individualized consideration and intellectual stimulation. Finally, we would also expect that leaders with a strong moral identity would be more likely to emphasize moral values in their decision making and communication with their subordinates, which again may be linked to the transformational facets of inspirational motivation (expectations) and idealized influence (Bass, 1998a, 1998b). For the same reason we would expect that a strong moral identity would be negatively associated with passive–avoidant behavior.

H4: High self-importance of moral identity (both symbolized and internalized) will be positively related to transformational behavior and negatively related to passive–avoidant behavior.

According to Rest (1986) people high on moral reasoning must also be motivated to act morally to implement moral thinking into behavior. Based on the suggested motivational effect of both symbolized and internalized moral identity on moral behavior (Aquino & Reed, 2002) we therefore postulate that a strong moral identity will augment the effect of moral reasoning on moral behavior, and explain more of the moral component of transformational leadership (Bass, 1998a, 1998b; Burns, 1978). Bass and Steidlmeier (1999) also emphasized morals as central in transactional leadership to gain trust and secure a fair contract regulating the exchange processes. From this we expect a similar augment effect as for transactional leadership, but weaker due to the more static nature of transactional leadership. In contrast, we expect moral identity to augment a negative correlation to passive–avoidant leadership (see Hypotheses 3 and 4).

H5: High self-importance of moral identity (symbolized and internalized) augments a positive correlation between postconventional moral schema and both transformational and transactional leadership, and a negative correlation toward passive–avoidant leadership.

METHOD

Sample

The participants in this study were first-year ($n = 95$), second-year ($n = 47$), and third-year ($n = 48$) cadets at the Norwegian Naval Academy (RNoNA). Mean age for the total sample ($N = 190$) was 24.6 years ($SD = 4.08$; range $= 20$–33 years), and 17 (9%) were women. The first academic year at the RNoNA is focused on leader-ship training, and the second and third years are devoted to branch-specific training with less emphasis on leader development. A total of 167 cadets (88%) responded to the survey. At the time of the data collection 8 cadets (4%) were absent on other duties, and 15 cadets (8%) chose not to participate. All participants had a minimum of 1 year of military service before entering the academy ($M = 2.3$ years), and they were all screened to ensure good physical and mental health, as well as cognitive aptitude, prior to admission.

Questionnaires

Defining Issues Test–2. The Defining Issues Test (DIT–2; Rest, 1979; Rest et al., 1999a, 1999b, 1999c) is designed to activate and measure the domi-nation of moral schemas. The test consists of five moral dilemmas with 12 moral arguments (items) attached to each. The items are typical representations of Kohlberg's stages of moral development (Stages 2–6). The respondent ranks the four most important arguments connected to each dilemma, which are scored 4, 3, 2, or 1 point(s) depending on whether they are ranked as the first, second, third, or fourth most important dilemma. These scores are again summarized across the three indexes used (see later), and transformed into percentage scores (from a minimum of 0% to a maximum of 95%).

To identify different forms of moral reasoning we indexed the three moral schemas (personal-interest, maintaining-norms and postconventional) according to Rest and coworkers (1999a). The postconventional (principled) score (P-score), is a representation of the respondent's preference for applying a postconventional moral schema (e.g., Kohlberg's Stages 5 and 6). The P-score has been considered the most significant index from the DIT over the last 25 years (Rest et al., 1999b). The maintaining-norms score (MN-score) is a representation of an individual's preference for moral thinking based on rules and regulations, operationalized as the maintaining-norms schema. Finally, the personal-interest score (PI-score) is a representation of an individual's preference for self-serving moral thinking, named the personal-interest schema. In this study, we use the unadjusted raw scores from these three dimensions to index different forms of moral reasoning (Turner et al., 2002).

The U.S. version of the DIT–2 is reported to have good psychometric character-istics with high levels of internal consistency (Cronbach's α from .78–.83) and well-established construct validity (Rest et al., 1999c). In this study we used a Nor-wegian translation, which was based on Bergem's (1985) Norwegian translation of the DIT–1. The internal consistency in this sample was weaker than for the U.S. samples (Cronbach's α from .67–.70. for the three index scores), but still at an acceptable level. The translation of the DIT–2 was done by bilingual translators using a back-translation procedure. To accommodate cultural differences, typical U.S. names have been altered into Norwegian ones in all cases, and in one case (Dilemma 4) the context was altered to create a Norwegian setting. Bergem reported a test–retest correlation in the mid-70s for the P-score ($r = .75$) on the first Norwegian version of the DIT–1. He also found that comparable Norwegian and U.S. samples scored at about the same levels. In a pilot study comparing P-scores from a sample ($N = 35$) of young ($M = 28$ years) Norwegian officers measured by the DIT–1 and the cadet sample used here measured by the DIT–2, no significant differences were revealed between the groups, indicating that the new Norwegian version of the DIT–2 is comparable to the older version of the test.

The Self-Importance of Moral Identity.   The Self-Importance of Moral Identity (Aquino & Reed, 2002) was used to measure the importance of moral traits to the officer's self-concept. The scale is two-dimensional and consists of 10 items scored on a Likert scale from 1 (*disagree strongly*) to 5 (*agree fully*). Five items measure symbolization, which is a representation of the public part of the moral self-concept (sample item: "The kinds of books and magazines that I read identify me as having these [moral] characteristics"), and 5 items measure internalization, which represents the private part of the moral self-concept (sample item: "Having these [moral] characteristics is an important part of myself"). Aquino and Reed reported a satisfactory construct validity and internal consistency. For the purpose of this study the measure was translated into Norwegian using a back-translation procedure. For the sample used here, Cronbach's alpha values were .71 and .74 for internalization and symbolization dimensions, respectively.

The Multifactor Leadership Questionnaire.   The Multifactor Leadership Questionnaire (MLQ–5X; Bass & Avolio, 1995), completed by peers, was used to evaluate leadership behavior. The MLQ questionnaire contains 45 items describing behavior and attributions, each rated on a 5-point scale ranging from 0 (*rarely*) to 4 (*to a large extent*). We used a Norwegian translation, produced through a back-translation procedure. In this study we extracted three outcome variables indexing transformational ($\alpha = .91$), transactional ($\alpha = .64$), and passive–avoidant ($\alpha = .78$) leadership behavior. In addition, facet scores for the three dimensions were also constructed. The transformational facets of idealized influence, inspirational motivation, intellectual stimulation, and individualized consideration revealed intercorrelations in the range of $r \geq .66$ and Cronbach's alpha $\geq .64$. Furthermore, the transactional facets of contingent rewards and management-by-exception–active revealed intercorrelations in the range of $r \geq .69$ and Cronbach's alpha $\geq .54$. Finally, the passive–avoidant facets of management-by-exception–passive and laissez-faire revealed intercorrelations in the range of $r \geq .69$ and Cronbach's alpha $\geq .58$. Permission was obtained from the MLQ developers to use their scale for the purpose of this research.

Procedure

The Navy Staff of Education and the RNoNA approved this study. All participants received written information and a briefing about the main purpose of the study. Participants were informed that participation was voluntary and that they could withdraw from the experiment at any time. Participants signed a declaration of consent, and completed the questionnaires on an individual basis. They were informed that the results were for research purposes, and that individual results would not be used in any performance assessment at the RNoNA. Data from the first-year cadets were collected after they had finished an 8-month extensive team-based leadership training (a combination of theory, coaching, and extensive exercises). Second-year cadets had finished a semester of branch-specific training, and third-year cadets had completed two additional semesters of branch-specific training. Leadership behavior was rated by peers, using a Norwegian translation of MLQ-5X (Bass & Avolio, 1995). The cadets operate in closely bonded squads during the first year of intensive leadership training, where they alternate as squad leaders and subordinates (Bartone, Johnsen, Eid, Brun, & Laberg, 2002). This experience gives them a thorough knowledge of each other in both leadership roles and as team members. The average number of peer raters in the cadet sample was 7.1 ($N = 1,186$). Data were manually transferred to SPSS 13.0 for statistical analyses and all questionnaires were coded to achieve anonymity.

Analyses

Cronbach's alpha and Pearson product–moment correlations were used as reliability measures. A 3 (transformational vs. transactional vs. passive–avoidant) × 3 (year class: 1 vs. 2 vs. 3) factorial design was used to control for systematic differences in leader behavior between the different cadet classes. Because no significant interaction effects emerged, data from all cohorts were pooled and treated as one group in the remaining analyses. In the subsequent analysis, self-ratings of moral reasoning and moral identity were entered in a block-wise hierarchical multiple regression analysis to predict leadership style, with transformational, transactional, and passive–avoidant styles as outcome variables. The independent variables were grouped in two blocks: moral reasoning measured by the DIT–2 index for personal-interest, rule-based, and postconventional moral reasoning; and moral identity measured by the internalization and symbolization index from the self-importance of moral identity measure. The variables in Blocks 1 and 2 were allowed to enter the equation if they fulfilled the inclusion criterion ($p < .05$).

RESULTS

Descriptive Statistics

Means, standard deviations, and Cronbach alpha values for the peer ratings of leadership style and self-ratings of moral reasoning and moral identity are shown in Table 1.

To explore Hypotheses 1 through 4, zero-order correlations were examined. The results in Table 1 reveal a strong positive correlation ($r = .76, p < .01$) between transformational and transactional behavior, whereas transformational and transactional leadership behavior correlated negatively ($r \geq -.55, p < .01$) with passive–avoidant leadership. Indicators of postconventional moral reasoning were positively correlated with transformational leadership behavior ($r = .27, p < .01$), and moral reasoning based on maintaining norms and personal interest was negatively correlated ($r \geq -.16, p < .05$) with transformational behavior. In addition, postconventional moral reasoning also correlated positively with transactional leader behavior ($r = .24, p < .01$), whereas moral reasoning based on maintaining norms and personal interest correlated negatively ($r \geq -.17, p < .05$) with transactional behavior. Furthermore, postconventional moral reasoning correlated negatively ($r = -.20, p < .05$) with passive–avoidant leadership behavior. Finally, internalization and symbolization of moral identity correlated positively ($r \geq .19, p < .05$) with transformational and transactional behavior, whereas symbolization of moral identity correlated negatively ($r = -.26, p < .01$) with passive–avoidant leader behavior.

Indicators of Moral Behavior and Leadership

The next series of analyses (i.e., Hypothesis 5) explored whether self-ratings of moral reasoning and moral identity might explain peer ratings of transformational, transactional, and passive–avoidant leadership behavior (see Table 2). To assess the potential influence of moral reasoning on leadership behavior, the following variables were entered into the equation in Step 1: personal-interest, rule-based, and postconventional moral reasoning. One objective of this study was to assess whether moral identity would predict leadership behavior better than moral reasoning in accordance with Aquino and Reed (2002). Thus in Step 2, controlling for moral reasoning, the unique contribution of internalized and symbolized moral identity on leadership behavior was determined.

Moral Behavior and Transformational Leadership

The results of the first equation revealed that postconventional moral reasoning explained 9% of the variance in transformational leadership, $F(3, 144) = 4.72, p <$

TABLE 1
Mean Scores, Standard Deviations, Cronbach's Alpha, and Pearson Correlations for Peer Ratings of Leadership Style, Self-Ratings of Moral Reasoning, and Moral Identity for the Navy Officer Cadets

Variables	M	SD	α	1	2	3	4	5	6	7	8
Leadership style											
1. Transformational	2.42	0.33	.91	—							
2. Transactional	2.20	0.28	.64	.76**	—						
3. Passive–avoidant	1.33	0.38	.78	-.71**	-.55**	—					
Moral reasoning											
4. Personal interests	24.64	11.47	.67	-.20*	-.17*	.08	—				
5. Maintaining norms	48.59	14.07	.70	-.16*	-.21**	.09	-.15	—			
6. Postconventional	36.48	14.45	.68	.27**	.24**	-.20*	-.36**	-.35	—		
Moral identity											
7. Internalization	4.41	0.45	.71	.19*	.15	-.05	-.03	.01	.12	—	
8. Symbolization	2.70	0.78	.74	.22**	.20*	-.26**	-.09	-.17*	.14	.30**	—

Note. $N = 147$.
*$p < .05$. **$p < .01$.

TABLE 2
Summary Table for Hierarchical Regression Analyses of Moral Reasoning
and Moral Identity Predicting Peer Ratings of Leadership Behavior
in Norwegian Navy Officer Cadets

	Transformational Leadership			Transactional Leadership			Passive–Avoidant Leadership		
	B	SE B	β	B	SE B	β	B	SE B	β
Step 1									
Personal interests	0.00	0.00	-.11	0.00	0.00	-.12	0.00	0.00	.01
Maintaining norms	0.00	0.00	-.04	0.00	0.00	-.12	0.00	0.00	.01
Postconventional	0.01	0.00	.23**	0.00	0.00	.18*	0.01	0.00	-.20*
	$\Delta R^2 = .09**$			$\Delta R^2 = .08**$			$\Delta R^2 = .04$		
Step 2									
Personal interests	0.00	0.00	-.11	0.00	0.00	-.12	0.00	0.00	-.02
Maintaining norms	0.00	0.00	-.04	0.00	0.00	-.12	0.00	0.00	-.03
Postconventional	0.01	0.00	.19*	0.00	0.00	.15	0.00	0.00	-.19*
Internalization	0.12	0.06	.16*	0.09	0.05	.14	0.02	0.07	.02
Symbolization	0.06	0.04	.13	0.04	0.03	.10	-0.12	0.42	-.24**
	$\Delta R^2 = .05*, R^2 = .14$			$\Delta R^2 = .04, R^2 = .12$			$\Delta R^2 = .05*, R^2 = .10$		

Note. N = 147.
*p < .05. **p < .01.

.01. In the second equation, controlling for the effects of moral reasoning, the factor of internalized moral identity contributed significantly to increasing the explained variance in transformational leadership by 5%. The result was a significant model, $F(5, 142) = 4.71, p < .01$, indicating that moral factors explained 14% of the variance in peer ratings of transformational leadership.

To follow up these findings, a new series of stepwise hierarchical regression analyses were performed with the four facets of transformational leadership as outcome variables. Descriptive statistics revealed that all facets of transformational leadership—that is, idealized influence ($M = 2.40, SD = .39$), inspirational motivation ($M = 2.44, SD = .36$), individualized consideration ($M = 2.51, SD = .36$), and intellectual stimulation ($M = 2.28, SD = .36$)—were positively intercorrelated ($r \geq .64, p > .01$).

Moral behavior and idealized influence.   In the first equation a significant model emerged, $F(3, 144) = 4.52, p < .01, R^2 = .09$, with postconventional moral reasoning as the only significant predictor variable ($\beta = .27, p < .01$). In the second equation, controlling for moral reasoning, a new significant model emerged, $F(5, 142) = 5.62, p < .01; \Delta R^2 = .08, p < .01; R^2 = .17, p < .01$, with postconventional moral reasoning ($\beta = .23, p < .01$) and symbolized moral identity ($\beta = .22, p < .01$) as the only significant predictor variables.

Moral predictors of inspirational motivation.   In the first equation a significant model emerged, $F(3, 144) = 4.77$, $p < .01$, $R^2 = .09$, with postconventional moral reasoning as a significant predictor variable ($\beta = .21$, $p < .01$). In the second equation, controlling for moral reasoning, a new significant model emerged, $F(5, 142) = 4.03$, $p < .01$; $\Delta R^2 = .03$; $R^2 = .12$, $p < .01$, with postconventional moral reasoning ($\beta = .18$, $p < .05$) as the only significant predictor variable.

Moral behavior and intellectual stimulation.   In the first and second equations (controlling for moral reasoning), no significant models emerged indicating that moral factors did not predict the transformational facet of intellectual stimulation.

Moral behavior and individualized consideration.   In the first equation a significant model emerged, $F(3, 144) = 5.64$, $p < .01$, $R^2 = .11$, with postconventional moral reasoning as the only significant predictor variable ($\beta = .24$, $p < .01$). In the second equation, controlling for moral reasoning, a new significant model emerged, $F(5, 142) = 5.51$, $p < .01$; $\Delta R^2 = .06$, $p < .01$; $R^2 = .16$, $p < .01$, with postconventional moral reasoning ($\beta = .19$, $p < .05$) and internalization of moral identity ($\beta = .21$, $p < .01$) as significant predictor variables.

Moral Behavior and Transactional Leadership

The results from the first equation (see Table 2) revealed a significant model, $F(3, 144) = 4.46$, $p < .01$, in which postconventional moral reasoning explained 8% of the variance in transactional leadership behavior. In the second equation, controlling for the effects of moral reasoning, none of the factors associated with moral identity contributed to the equation. In the final model, $F(5, 142) = 3.93$, $p < .01$, indicators of moral behavior explained 12% of the variance in transactional leadership behavior.

Subsequently, a new series of stepwise hierarchical regression analyses were performed with the two facets of transactional leadership. Descriptive statistics revealed that the facets of transactional leadership—that is, contingent reward ($M = 2.44$, $SD = .32$) and management-by-exception–active ($M = 2.05$, $SD = .28$)—were positively intercorrelated ($r = .48$, $p > .01$).

Moral behavior and contingent reward.   In the first equation a significant model emerged, $F(3, 144) = 3.23$, $p < .05$, $R^2 = .06$. In the second equation, controlling for moral reasoning, a new significant model emerged, $F(5, 142) = 3.39$, $p < .01$; $\Delta R^2 = .04$, $p < .05$; $R^2 = .11$, $p < .01$, with symbolization of moral identity ($\beta = .17$, $p < .05$) as the only significant predictor variable.

Moral behavior and management-by-exception–active. In the first and second equations (controlling for moral reasoning), no significant models emerged.

Moral Behavior and Passive–Avoidant Leadership

The results from the first equation (see Table 2) produced no significant model. In the second equation, controlling for moral reasoning, symbolization of moral identity and postconventional moral reasoning contributed significantly to increasing the explained variance in passive–avoidant leadership by 5%. In the final model, $F(5, 142) = 3.03, p < .01$, indicators of moral behavior explained 10% of the variance in passive–avoidant leadership behavior.

These results were followed up in a new series of stepwise hierarchical regression analyses with the two facets of passive–avoidant leadership behavior as outcome variables. Descriptive statistics revealed that management-by-exception–passive ($M = 1.55, SD = .36$) and laissez-faire ($M = 1.15, SD = .46$) were positively correlated ($r = .71, p > .01$).

Moral behavior and management-by-exception–passive. The first equation did not produce any significant model. In the second equation, controlling for moral reasoning, a significant model emerged, $F(5, 142) = 2.42, p < .05; \Delta R^2 = .06, p < .01; R^2 = .08, p < .05$, with symbolization of moral identity ($\beta = -.25, p < .01$) as a significant predictor variable.

Moral behavior and laissez-faire. In the first equation a significant model emerged, $F(3, 144) = 2.82, p < .05, R^2 = .06$, with postconventional moral reasoning as a significant predictor variable ($\beta = -.24, p < .01$. In the second equation, controlling for moral reasoning, a new significant model emerged, $F(5, 142) = 2.89, p < .05; \Delta R^2 = .04; R^2 = .09, p < .01$, with postconventional moral reasoning ($\beta = -.23, p < .05$) and symbolization of moral identity ($\beta = -.20, p < .05$) as significant predictor variables.

DISCUSSION

This study is the first empirical assessment of the relation between indicators of moral behavior and peer ratings of leadership behavior in a military sample. This exploratory study is an important first step in a more systematical analysis of the influence of moral behavior on military leadership and performance in operational settings.

The findings of this study are in line with or give partial support to Hypotheses 1, 3, and 4 in indicating that postconventional moral reasoning and moral identity were positively related to transformational leadership behavior, and both were negatively related to passive–avoidant leadership. These results support Turner et al.'s (2002) findings that postconventional moral reasoning relates to transformational leadership. A unique finding of this study is that indicators of moral identity were also significantly related to transformational leadership. These findings support Burns's (1978) and Bass's (1998a) emphasis on moral competence as a precondition to transformational leadership, and show that the level of moral reasoning of Norwegian officers and the importance they attach to moral values in their self-concept do influence their ability to stand out as transformational leaders.

Contrary to our expectations in Hypothesis 2, we did not find an association between moral reasoning based on the maintaining-norms schema and transactional behavior. One possible explanation for this might be that whereas the maintaining-norms schema is oriented toward maintaining existing rules and regulations to avoid chaos, the contingent reward factor is more dynamic in its nature, involving the process of establishing consensus between different stakeholders as a "contract" regulating cooperation (Bass & Steidlmeier, 1999). This consensus building may demand more complex moral thinking, which again may explain why transactional leadership, and contingent reward in particular, relates positively to postconventional reasoning.

This study did lend support to Hypothesis 5 in revealing that the self-importance of moral identity did augment the effects of moral reasoning in explaining leadership behavior. This seems to support Rest's (1986) claim that moral behavior is a result of several psychological processes that interact, and that cognitive-developmental approaches should be supplemented with social psychological approaches to better predict moral behavior. The results also indicate that moral reasoning should be connected to the self-concept, to strengthen the link to moral action (Aquino & Reed, 2002). Further, the results support Turner et al.'s (2002) and Price's (2003) claims that research on moral issues and transformational leadership should include a variety of moral variables.

According to Hypothesis 5, indicators of moral behavior explained between 9% and 12% of the variance in passive–avoidant, transactional, and transformational leader behavior. This finding is quite interesting, given that previous studies on Norwegian leaders by and large have had little success in predicting leadership behavior from personality traits (Hetland & Sandal, 2003). It appears that moral behavior would be a fruitful variable in future studies of individual differences in leader behavior.

It is interesting to note that indicators of moral behavior emerged as significant predictor variables for the transformational facets of idealized influence (17%), inspirational motivation (12%), and individualized consideration (16%; Hypotheses 1 and 4). This indicates that the military culture values leaders that can reason on moral issues on a principled level, and who also see morals as an important aspect of their own identity. However, somewhat surprisingly, moral behavior did not seem to be related to the intellectual stimulation facet. One possible explanation might be that this component is more technically and intellectually oriented. The result may also stem from sample characteristics; the mean score on intellectual stimulation is significantly lower ($t \geq 5.3$, $p < .01$) than on the other transformational factors. This may indicate that the cadets are less oriented toward intellectual reasoning in general, which again could weaken the link to moral reasoning. It would be interesting to replicate this study in another sample with higher scores on intellectual stimulation.

We also found support for Hypothesis 1 that both the maintaining-norms and the personal-interest schema are negatively related to transformational leadership. This may indicate that these more rigid and self-oriented moral schemas do not fully capture the moral challenges that transformational leaders have to deal with.

It is worth noticing that the moral identity factor of symbolization seems to represent a significant factor in explaining all the global leadership factors (Hypothesis 4), whereas internalization only loads on transformational leadership. This may be due to the explicit nature of the symbolism construct, emphasizing a visible and assertive moral orientation, which again may facilitate trust and admiration, two core aspects of idealized influence.

Finally, and in accordance with Hypotheses 3 and 4, moral behavior was negatively related to passive–avoidant leadership on both facets, management-by-exception–passive (8%) and laissez-faire (9%). Our findings indicate that this shortcoming in fulfilling leadership responsibilities may stem partly from a lack of moral competency. We suggest that a limited ability to reason on moral issues in a principled and unbiased way may influence the leader's ability to see his or her leadership responsibility in a moral perspective, again causing low commitment to leadership. We further suggest that when moral values are of low personal importance, it becomes emotionally easy to ignore one's leader responsibilities, not activating any self-regulatory mechanisms in response to moral shortcomings. On the other hand, unexpectedly (Hypothesis 3), the personal-interest index was not related to lack of leadership. The explanation for this may be that this schema is oriented toward self-interest, which, when applied to a leadership role, actually may entail active leadership. This active, self-serving approach may compensate underdeveloped perspective-taking abilities (Kuhnert & Lewis, 1987).

Some possible limitations to this study deserve mentioning. First of all we acknowledge that the relatively small sample of military cadets means that the findings may not apply to other organizations, or across gender. However, the homogeneous nature of this sample of Norwegian naval cadets might also be seen as a possible advantage because previous research on moral development has argued that an individual's age, education, and gender are related to moral reasoning levels (Gilligan, 1982; Rest & Narvaez, 1994). Second, it would be desirable for similar studies in the future to include measures of individual differences in personality traits to control for possible effects of interaction between personality measures and indicators of moral behavior.

This study offers strong preliminary support for the idea that although moral behavior is seen as a core value in itself, it is also intimately linked to leadership behavior in military leaders. In highlighting the significance of moral behavior in leaders, this study expands this field by showing that specific indicators of moral behavior are linked to certain facets of transformational and transactional leadership behavior. Given the clearly articulated moral nature of the tasks that military officers are confronted with during military operations, these findings may have significant implications for leader development, mentoring, and character-building programs. Finally, this study extends previously published data by showing an association between indicators of moral behavior and passive–avoidant leadership behavior. Passive avoidance can be highly dysfunctional and in an operational setting it might also jeopardize an entire mission (Taguba, 2004). Therefore, the ability to predict passive–avoidant leadership behavior would have particular value in operational settings. Because moral reasoning and moral identity are identifiable and can be assessed in individuals prior to their exposure to command, tests such as this might be useful when trying to identify individuals who may be likely to emerge as dysfunctional leaders in operational settings.

ACKNOWLEDGMENT

We thank Odd Arne Nissestad for advice and help in the collection of data.

REFERENCES

Aquino, K., & Reed, A. (2002). The self-importance of moral identity. *Journal of Personality and Social Psychology, 83,* 1423–1440.

Avolio, B. J., Bass, B. M., & Jung, D. 1. (1999). Re-examining the components of transformational and transactional leadership using the multifactor leadership questionnaire. *Journal of Occupational and Organizational Psychology, 72,* 441–462.

Bailey, F. G. (1988). *Humbuggery and manipulation: The art of leadership.* Ithaca, NY: Cornell University Press.

Bartone, P. T. (2004). Understanding prisoner abuse at Abu Ghraib: Psychological considerations and leadership implications. *The Military Psychologist, 20,* 12–16.

Bartone, P. T., Johnsen, B. H., Eid, J., Brun, W., & Laberg, J. C. (2002). Factors influencing small unit cohesion in Norwegian Navy officer cadets. *Military Psychology, 14,* 1–22.

Bass, B. M. (1985). *Leadership and performance beyond expectations.* New York: The Free Press.

Bass, B. M. (1998a). The ethics of transformational leadership. In J. Ciulla (Ed.), *Ethics: The heart of leadership* (pp. 169–192). Westport, CT: Praeger.

Bass, B. M. (1998b). *Transformational leadership: Industrial, military, and educational impact.* Mahwah, NJ: Lawrence Erlbaum Associates, Inc.

Bass, B. M., & Avolio, B. J. (1995). *Transformational leadership development: Manual for the Multifactor Leadership Questionnaire.* Palo Alto, CA: Consulting Psychologists Press.

Bass, B. M., & Avolio, B. J. (2000). *Platoon readiness as a function of leadership, platoon and company cultures.* Binghamton, NY: Research Foundation of the State University of New York, Office of Research Sponsored Programs.

Bass, B. M., Avolio, B. J., Jung, D. I., & Beson, Y. (2003). Predicting unit performance by assessing transformational and transactional leadership. *Journal of Applied Psychology, 88,* 207–218.

Bass, B. M., & Steidlmeier, P. (1999). Ethics, character, and authentic transformational leadership behavior. *Leadership Quarterly, 10,* 181–217.

Bergem, T. (1985). *Sakens kjerne: Manual* [Defining issues test: Norwegian manual]. Bergen, Norway: NLA-Forlaget.

Blasi, A. (1980). Bridging moral cognition and moral action: A critical review of the literature. *Psychological Bulletin, 88,* 1–45.

Blasi, A. (1984). Moral identity: Its role in moral functioning. In W. Kurtines & J. Gewirtz (Eds.), *Morality, moral behavior, and moral development* (pp. 128–139). New York: Wiley.

Burns, J. M. (1978). *Leadership.* New York: Harper & Row.

Ciulla, J. (Ed.). (1998). *Ethics: The heart of leadership.* Westport, CT: Praeger.

Conger, J. A., & Kanungo, R. A. (1988). *Charismatic leadership: The elusive factor in organization effectiveness.* San Francisco: Jossey-Bass.

Den Hartog, Van Muijen, J. J., & Koopman, P. L. (1997). Transactional versus transformational leadership: An analysis of the MLQ. *Journal of Occupational and Organizational Psychology, 70,* 255–267.

Department of the Army. (2004). *Field manual—Interim, No. 3–07.22.* Washington, DC: Author.

Dukerich, J. M., Nichols, M. L., Elm, D. R., & Vollrath, D. A. (1990). Moral reasoning in groups: Leaders make a difference. *Human Relations, 43,* 473–493.

Eid, J., Johnsen, B. H., Brun, W., Laberg, J. C., Larsson, G., & Nyhus, J. K. (2004). Situational awareness and transformational leadership: An exploratory study. *Military Psychology, 16,* 203–209.

Gardner, J. (1990). *On leadership.* New York: The Free Press.

Gibbs, J. C. (2004). *Moral development and reality: Beyond the theories of Kohlberg and Hoffman.* Thousand Oaks, CA: Sage.

Gilligan, C. (1982). *In a different voice: Psychological theory and women's development.* Cambridge, MA: Harvard University Press.

Hetland, H., & Sandal, G. M. (2003). Transformational leadership in Norway: Outcomes and personality correlates. *European Journal of Work and Organizational Psychology, 12,* 147–170.

King, P. M., & Mayhew, M. J. (2002). Moral judgement development in higher education: Insights from the Defining Issues Test. *Journal of Moral Education, 31,* 247–270.

Kohlberg, L. (1984). *Essays on moral development: Vol. 2. The psychology of moral development: The nature and validity of moral stages.* San Francisco: Harper & Row.

Kuhnert, K. W., & Lewis, P. (1987). Transactional and transformational leadership: A constructive/developmental analysis. *Academy of Management Review, 4,* 648–657.

Lowe, K., Kroeck, K. G., & Sivasubrahmaniam, N. (1996). Effectiveness correlates of transformational and transactional leadership: A meta-analytic review. *Leadership Quarterly, 7,* 385–425.

Popper, M., & Mayseless, O. (2003). Back to basics: Applying a parenting perspective to transformational leadership. *Leadership Quarterly, 14,* 41–65.

Price, T. L. (2003). The ethics of authentic transformational leadership. *Leadership Quarterly, 14,* 67–81.

Rawles, J. (1971). *A theory of justice.* Cambridge, MA: Harvard University Press.

Rest, J. (1979). *Development in judging moral issues.* Minneapolis: University of Minnesota Press.

Rest, J. (1986). *Moral development: Advances in research and theory.* New York: Praeger.

Rest, J., & Narvaez, D. (1994). *Moral development in the professions: Psychology and applied ethics.* Hillsdale, NJ: Lawrence Erlbaum Associates, Inc.

Rest, J., Narvaez, D., Bebeau, M., & Thoma, S. (1999a). DIT2: Devising and testing a new instrument of moral judgment. *Journal of Educational Psychology, 91,* 644–659.

Rest, J., Narvaez, D., Bebeau, M., & Thoma, S. (1999b). A Neo-Kohlbergian approach: The DIT and schema theory. *Educational Psychology Review, 11,* 291–324.

Rest, J., Narvaez, D., Bebeau, M. J., & Thoma, S. J. (1999c). *Postconventional moral thinking: A Neo-Kohlbergian approach.* Mahwah, NJ: Lawrence Erlbaum Associates, Inc.

Stevens, C. U., D'Intio, R. S., & Victor, B. (1995). The moral quandary of transformational leadership: Change for whom? *Research in Organizational Change and Development, 8,* 123–143.

Taguba, A. M. (2004). *Article 15-6 investigation of the 800th Military Police Brigade.* Retrieved May 30, 2005, from http://www.agonist.org/annex/taguba.htm

Turner, N., Barling, J., Epitropaki, O., Butcher, V., & Milner, C. (2002). Transformational leadership and moral reasoning. *Journal of Applied Psychology, 87,* 304–311.

U.S. Marine Corps. (1997). *Warfighting: MCDP 1.* Washington, DC: Department of the Navy.

Waldman, D. A., Bass, B. M., & Yammarino, F. J. (1990). Adding to contingent-reward behavior: The augmenting effect of charismatic leadership. *Group & Organizational Studies, 15,* 381–394.

Weber, M. (1947). *The theory of social and economic organizations* (T. Parson, Trans.). New York: The Free Press. (Original work published in 1924)

MILITARY PSYCHOLOGY, 2006, *18*(Suppl.), S57–S68

Character Strengths and Virtues of Developing Military Leaders: An International Comparison

Michael D. Matthews
Department of Behavioral Sciences and Leadership
U.S. Military Academy

Jarle Eid
Department of Psychosocial Science
University of Bergen, Norway
and the Royal Norwegian Navy

Dennis Kelly
Office of Institutional Research
U.S. Military Academy

Jennifer K. S. Bailey
Department of Behavioral Sciences and Leadership
U.S. Military Academy

Christopher Peterson
Department of Psychology
University of Michigan

Positive character strengths, virtues, and values are touted in military doctrine as critical for effective leadership, yet little evidence exists describing such traits in military samples. This study compared West Point cadets ($N = 103$), Norwegian Naval Academy cadets ($N = 141$), and U.S. civilians aged 18 to 21 ($N = 838$) with respect to 24 character strengths. Results generally showed that the absolute scores of West Point cadets were higher than either of the other 2 groups. However, when the rank orders of character strengths were compared, the 2 military samples were more highly correlated with each other than either was with the U.S. civilian sample. The greatest

Correspondence should be addressed to Michael D. Matthews, Department of Behavioral Sciences and Leadership, U.S. Military Academy, West Point, NY 10096. E-mail: Mike.Matthews@usma.edu

strengths evident among the military samples were honesty, hope, bravery, industry, and teamwork. Implications for multiforce military operations are discussed.

Positive psychology represents a novel conceptual framework from which to view the development of military leaders. This approach focuses on enhancing human strengths rather than eliminating weaknesses (Peterson & Seligman, 2004). Military personnel represent a relatively young, physically fit, and emotionally stable population. Thus, the principles of positive psychology seem most appropriate for understanding factors that affect how they might develop and behave as leaders. The work reported here represents the initial findings of an ongoing research project aimed at describing character strengths and virtues of military personnel and identifying which of these are most critical to successful adaptation to the stressors and demands of military life and operational requirements.

Peterson and Seligman (2004) described in depth the origin of positive psychology and the development of a classification scheme of 24 character strengths and virtues that they suggested are ubiquitously valued across cultures. Virtues represent "core characteristics valued by moral philosophers and religious thinkers" (Peterson & Seligman, 2004, p. 13) and are thought to be universal in the human species. Character strengths are "the psychological ingredients—processes or mechanisms—that define virtues" (p. 13). Specifically, these "ingredient" character strengths are grouped into the six core moral virtues that emerged from Peterson and Seligman's extensive analysis of the psychological, religious, and philosophical literature. The six virtues and their component character strengths are (a) wisdom and knowledge (creativity, curiosity, open-mindedness, love of learning, and perspective), (b) courage (bravery, persistence, integrity, and vitality), (c) humanity (love, kindness, and social intelligence), (d) justice (citizenship, fairness, and leadership), (e) temperance (forgiveness and mercy, humility, prudence, and self-regulation), and (f) transcendence (appreciation of beauty and excellence, gratitude, hope, humor, and spirituality; Peterson & Seligman, 2004, pp. 29–30).

With regard to military psychology, however, positive psychology has a long past but only a short history (to paraphrase Ebbinghaus; see Boring, 1950, p. ix). Military doctrine has long asserted that character and values are critical to successful military leadership, although few empirical studies address this assertion, with none to date from the perspective of positive psychology. For example, U.S. Army doctrine, as expressed in Field Manual 22-100, explicitly names seven core values of overriding importance in leadership: loyalty, duty, respect, selfless service, honor, integrity, and personal courage (U.S. Department of the Army, 1999, p. B-2). Four of these values—loyalty, respect, integrity, and personal courage—are among the 24 core character strengths and virtues identified by Peterson and Seligman (2004, pp. 29–30), specifically citizenship, fairness, integrity, and bravery. It is worth noting that military doctrine does not offer operational definitions of character or values. Thus, discussions of these constructs from a doctrinal perspective may not compare directly to the formal constructs of virtues and strengths as defined by Peterson and Seligman.

A close reading of Field Manual 22-100 reveals additional characteristics of the ideal Army leader that are reflected in the strengths and virtues enumerated by Peterson and Seligman (2004). Desired mental abilities of Army leaders include self-discipline, judgment, and cultural awareness (U.S. Department of the Army, 1999, p. B-3). These correspond to the positive psychology strengths of self-regulation, open-mindedness, and social intelligence (Peterson & Seligman, 2004, p. 29). Emotional attributes valued by the Army include maintaining a positive attitude, akin to the character strength of hope or optimism. The interpersonal skill of empowering subordinates relates to the character strength of leadership. Conceptual skills attributes listed by doctrine include creative thinking (creativity) and critical reasoning (open-mindedness). Other key Army leader attributes and their corresponding positive psychology character strengths include "taking care of subordinates and their families" (kindness), "recognize and generate innovative solutions" (creativity), "promote teamwork and achievement" (citizenship), and "continue to function under adverse conditions" (persistence). Thus, at least half of the 24 character strengths and values identified by Peterson and Seligman are explicitly mentioned in Army leadership doctrine.

Although Army doctrine is clear in stating the importance of character in officer development, relatively little empirical research has been reported that systematically assesses such characteristics among military personnel or, perhaps more important, determines their predictive validity with respect to relevant outcome variables.[1] Bartone, Snook, and Tremble (2002) examined the relation among several cognitive and personality variables on the leader performance of West Point cadets. They reported that social judgment skills and logical reasoning, as well as the personality traits of agreeableness and conscientiousness, moderately predicted military performance grades. Kelly, Matthews, and Bartone (2005), in another study of West Point cadets, reported that hardiness predicted military performance and attrition from West Point, and Murray and Johnson (2001) reported that the Myers-Briggs Type Indicator was, in general, a good predictor of both academic and military success at the U.S. Naval Academy. Gough, Lazzari, Fioravanti, and Stracca (1978) administered the 300-item Adjective Check List to West Point cadets, showing that cadet self-ratings of conscientiousness, self-discipline, and goal-directedness predicted better military performance. Gibb (1947), in a study of

---

[1]This is not to say there is any dearth of research on general intrapersonal factors related to leadership in the military or the civilian sector. Our intent is not to minimize the value of these contributions by failing to review this literature, but space limitations require us to focus on the application of positive psychology principles to leader development and behavior. The reader may refer to Yukl (2002), Zaccaro (2001), or many other sources for thorough reviews of the more general literature.

Australian Army officers, found that more successful officers were self-confident and highly sociable. Finally, Eid, Matthews, Johnsen, and Meland (2005) reported that dispositional optimism was negatively correlated with self-reported situation awareness in a combat leadership course.

This study is part of a collaborative effort between researchers at the U.S. Military Academy (West Point) and the Royal Norwegian Naval Academy (RNA) designed to explore systematically the role of positive psychology factors, including the 24 character strengths identified and defined by Peterson and Seligman (2004), and related constructs in the adjustment and performance of military personnel under stressful conditions. The mission of military academies is to develop future leaders. West Point and the RNA share this goal, which importantly entails the nurturing of the dimensions of character thought to be important in leading soldiers or sailors in military operations and in adjusting to the rigors of military life. Although character strengths and virtues presented by Peterson and Seligman are hypothesized to be universal, they may well indeed vary in importance or magnitude across groups and cultures. These differences may also influence leader behavior and decision making in multinational operations. The purpose of this study was to assess and compare the 24 character strengths identified by Peterson and Seligman in first-year West Point cadets and RNA cadets. For context, responses of the two military samples were also compared to a large sample of U.S. respondents of similar age and education.

METHOD

Participants

Three different groups of respondents were included in the study. Because the military samples included relatively small numbers of women respondents, the current analyses included only the responses of men. There were 103 West Point cadets (M age = 18.3 years, range = 18–22 years), 141 RNA cadets (M age = 25.31 years, SD = 4.35), and 838 U.S. respondents from 18 to 21 years old who had completed some college work. The West Point cadets were volunteers from the freshman class who entered West Point in 2004, and were given extra course credit for their participation. All RNA cadets entering RNA in 2003 and 2004 were tested. The U.S. civilian sample was obtained from a database maintained by the Values in Action Web site (www.viastrengths.org).

Survey

The Values in Action Inventory of Strengths (VIA–IS) was used to assess character strengths and values. The development and initial validation of the VIA–IS was described in detail by Peterson and Seligman (2004, pp. 627–633). The measure includes 24 scales, each consisting of 10 items with a 5-point response option asking respondents to indicate to what extent (*very much like me, like me, neutral, unlike me,* or *very much unlike me*) a particular statement (e.g., "I find the world an interesting place") is representative of them. Peterson and Seligman reported that all 24 scales have alpha values exceeding .70. Test–retest correlations over a 4-month period are approximately .70. As explained, the 24 scales are grouped into six core moral virtues.

Procedure

At West Point, volunteers from the freshman class were solicited from a general psychology course early in their first semester of study. Testing occurred in a group setting using a paper-and-pencil version of the VIA–IS. All respondents completed the VIA–IS in less than 1 hr.

At the RNA, volunteer cadets were solicited from the leadership course during their first semester at the academy. Testing occurred in a group setting using a paper-and-pencil version of the original U.S. version of the VIA–IS. Although the questionnaire was not translated into Norwegian, language proficiency did not seem to represent any problem, and all respondents completed the VIA–IS in about 1 hr. The U.S. civilian sample completed the VIA–IS individually by logging on to the Values in Action Web site. These respondents were unsolicited volunteers. For the current study, only responses from those who indicated their age was between 18 and 21, inclusive, and who reported completing some college were analyzed.

RESULTS

Comparisons of Mean Differences Between Groups

Means and standard deviations for each of the three comparison groups for the six core moral virtues are shown in Table 1. A 3 (group) × 6 (core virtue) analysis of variance (ANOVA) showed a main effect for group, $F(2, 1079) = 16.0, p < .001$. A main effect for core virtue was also significant, $F(5, 5395) = 77.05, p < .001$, as was the interaction between core virtue and group, $F(10, 5395) = 14.96, p < .001$.

Post hoc analyses using Tukey's honestly significant difference test ($df = 2$, 3522, $\alpha = .05$), also summarized in Table 1, showed that the West Point sample rated themselves higher than the Norwegian cadets on all six of the core moral virtues, and higher than the U.S. civilian samples on courage, justice, and temperance. The Norwegian Naval cadets rated themselves lower than the U.S. civilian group on wisdom and knowledge, humanity, and transcendence. No significant differences were found between the RNA and the U.S. sample on the core moral

TABLE 1
Means and Standard Deviations of Comparison Groups
on Six Moral Virtues

	RNA		West Point		U.S. Civilians	
Moral Virtue	M	SD	M	SD	M	SD
Wisdom and knowledge	3.62$_a$	0.35	3.89$_b$	0.44	3.78$_b$	0.47
Courage	3.75$_a$	0.34	4.01$_b$	0.39	3.69$_a$	0.51
Humanity	3.76$_a$	0.33	3.98$_b$	0.47	3.84$_b$	0.52
Justice	3.71$_a$	0.36	3.93$_b$	0.49	3.72$_a$	0.52
Temperance	3.48$_a$	0.28	3.71$_b$	0.44	3.47$_a$	0.48
Transcendence	3.36$_a$	0.37	3.87$_b$	0.50	3.68$_b$	0.53

Note. Means in the same row that do not share subscripts differ at $p < .05$ in the Tukey honestly significant difference comparison. RNA = Royal Norwegian Naval Academy.

virtues of courage, justice, and temperance. West Point cadets rated themselves higher than U.S. civilians on courage, justice, and temperance.

Descriptive statistics for the three groups across all 24 individual character strengths and virtues are summarized in Table 2. A 3 (group) × 24 (character strength) ANOVA showed a significant main effect for group, $F(2, 1079) = 15.86$, $p < .001$. The main effect for character strength was also significant, $F(23, 24817) = 95.80$, $p < .001$, as was the interaction between group and character strength, $F(46, 24817) = 15.75$, $p < .001$.

Paired comparisons among the three groups for each of the 24 strengths, also summarized in Table 2, reveal that West Point cadets rated themselves higher than Norwegian cadets on 22 of the 24 assessed items, with no significant difference between West Point and Norwegian cadets on forgiveness and zest. West Point cadets rated themselves significantly higher than U.S. civilians on the following strengths: bravery, prudence, teamwork, curiosity, fairness, honesty, hope, industry, leadership, modesty, self-control, social intelligence, and spirituality. U.S. civilians rated themselves higher than West Point cadets on only one character strength: beauty. There were no differences between West Point cadets and U.S. civilians on capacity to love, creativity, forgiveness, gratitude, humor, judgment, kindness, love of learning, perspective, or zest.

Comparisons between Norwegian cadets and U.S. civilians showed the Norwegian cadets rated themselves lower on the following 13 character strengths: beauty, capacity to love, creativity, gratitude, humor, judgment, kindness, leadership, love of learning, modesty, perspective, social intelligence, and spirituality. Norwegian cadets rated themselves higher on only one character strength: self-control. There were no differences between Norwegian cadets and U.S. civilians on 10 character strengths: bravery, prudence, teamwork, curiosity, fairness, forgiveness, honesty, hope, industry, and zest.

TABLE 2
Means and Standard Deviations of Comparison Groups
Across 24 Character Strengths

Strength	RNA		West Point		U.S. Civilian	
	M	SD	M	SD	M	SD
Beauty	3.00$_a$	0.56	3.42$_b$	0.68	3.67$_c$	0.71
Bravery	3.65$_a$	0.42	4.05$_b$	0.50	3.66$_a$	0.63
Love	3.76$_a$	0.47	3.97$_b$	0.63	3.98$_b$	0.63
Prudence	3.31$_a$	0.42	3.52$_b$	0.64	3.40$_a$	0.63
Teamwork	3.74$_a$	0.38	4.02$_b$	0.50	3.78$_a$	0.54
Creativity	3.56$_a$	0.49	3.77$_b$	0.64	3.70$_b$	0.66
Curiosity	3.85$_a$	0.46	4.02$_b$	0.50	3.86$_a$	0.56
Fairness	3.78$_a$	0.39	3.99$_b$	0.55	3.85$_a$	0.53
Forgiveness	3.52$_a$	0.39	3.45$_a$	0.72	3.50$_a$	0.70
Gratitude	3.43$_a$	0.44	3.95$_b$	0.44	3.86$_b$	0.61
Honesty	3.89$_a$	0.36	4.12$_b$	0.48	3.98$_a$	0.49
Hope	3.82$_a$	0.45	4.05$_b$	0.57	3.76$_a$	0.65
Humor	3.78$_a$	0.49	4.00$_b$	0.69	4.00$_b$	0.58
Industry	3.76$_a$	0.47	4.09$_b$	0.51	3.64$_a$	0.66
Judgment	3.69$_a$	0.41	3.99$_b$	0.47	3.88$_b$	0.52
Kindness	3.85$_a$	0.37	4.00$_b$	0.55	4.06$_b$	0.51
Leadership	3.54$_a$	0.51	3.86$_b$	0.55	3.73$_c$	0.55
Love of learning	3.23$_a$	0.51	3.54$_b$	0.64	3.49$_b$	0.69
Modesty	3.20$_a$	0.40	3.64$_b$	0.62	3.34$_c$	0.63
Perspective	3.66$_a$	0.42	3.93$_b$	0.54	3.82$_b$	0.53
Self-control	3.54$_a$	0.42	3.80$_b$	0.48	3.31$_c$	0.62
Social intelligence	3.68$_a$	0.41	3.95$_b$	0.53	3.81$_c$	0.55
Spirituality	2.75$_a$	0.82	3.89$_b$	0.85	3.54$_c$	0.87
Zest	3.60$_a$	0.45	3.64$_a$	0.54	3.60$_a$	0.63

Note. Means in the same row that do not share subscripts differ at $p < .05$ in the Tukey honestly significant difference comparison. RNA = Royal Norwegian Naval Academy.

Comparison of Rank Orderings Between Groups

Because of the existence of possible cultural differences between U.S. and Norwegian respondents in terms of how self-report rating scales might be used, a comparison of the rank orders of the six moral virtues and the 24 character strengths was made. Table 3 shows the rank ordering of the six moral virtues for the three samples. With the exception of courage, which was ranked higher for the two military samples, and for wisdom, which was higher for the U.S. civilian sample, there was substantial similarity among the three sets of rankings.

In comparing the rankings of the three samples for all 24 character strengths, as displayed in Table 4, it appears that there is much more similarity among the samples than suggested by a parametric analysis of mean differences. Indeed, there

TABLE 3
Rank Ordering of the Six Moral Virtues by Sample

RNA	West Point	U.S. Civilians
Humanity (1)	Courage (1)	Humanity (1)
Courage (2)	Humanity (2)	Wisdom (2)
Justice (3)	Justice (3)	Justice (3)
Wisdom (4)	Wisdom (4)	Courage (4)
Temperance (5)	Transcendence (5)	Transcendence (5)
Transcendence (6)	Temperance (6)	Temperance (6)

Note.   RNA = Royal Norwegian Naval Academy.

was a significant correlation between the rank order of strengths between the Norwegian and West Point samples, Spearman's $r = .82$, $t(22) = 6.81$, $p < .001$; between the Norwegian and U.S. civilian sample, Spearman's $r = .74$, $t(22) = 5.14$, $p < .001$; and between the West Point and U.S. civilian samples, Spearman's $r = .61$, $t(22) = 3.58$, $p < .01$.

DISCUSSION

These data represent the first empirical assessment among military samples of the 24 character strengths and virtues postulated by Peterson and Seligman (2004). This descriptive analysis is an important first step in systematically analyzing the impact of these strengths and values on military leadership and performance. The data suggest that Americans attracted to attend a service academy display a set of values consistent with U.S. military doctrine (U.S. Department of the Army, 1999) and the West Point officer development model, with character strengths of honesty, bravery, teamwork, industry, and fairness among their top 10 character strengths. Although an analysis based on comparison of means suggested substantial differences in character strengths among the three samples, and particularly between West Point cadets and Norwegian cadets, a comparison based on rank ordering of the character strengths suggests these two groups have much more in common than what is suggested by the comparison of absolute means. Indeed, West Point and Norwegian cadets are more similar in their rank ordering of character strengths than were either group with respect to the U.S. civilians. This overall pattern of substantial overlap among character strengths and virtues in the two military samples suggests that soldiers, despite obvious cultural differences, may share a common bond of values that may work in their favor in executing multinational operations.

However, sometimes even subtle differences may be important in multinational military operations. The two military samples correlated highly, but not perfectly. For example, spirituality was ranked last among the 24 character strengths by the

TABLE 4
Rank Ordering of 24 Character Strengths by Sample

RNA	West Point	U.S. Civilians
Honesty (1)	Honesty (1)	Kindness (1)
Kindness (2)	Industry (2)	Humor (2)
Curiosity (3)	Hope (3)	Honesty (3.5)
Hope (4)	Bravery (4)	Love (3.5)
Humor (5)	Curiosity (5.5)	Judgment (5)
Fairness (6)	Teamwork (5.5)	Gratitude (6.5)
Industry (7)	Kindness (7)	Curiosity (6.5)
Love (8.5)	Humor (8)	Fairness (8)
Teamwork (8.5)	Judgment (9)	Perspective (9)
Judgment (10)	Fairness (10)	Social intelligence (10)
Social intelligence (11)	Love (11)	Teamwork (11)
Perspective (12)	Gratitude (12.5)	Hope (12)
Bravery (13)	Social intelligence (12.5)	Leadership (13)
Zest (14)	Perspective (14)	Creativity (14)
Creativity (15)	Spirituality (15.5)	Beauty (15)
Self-control (16)	Leadership (15.5)	Bravery (16)
Leadership (17.5)	Self-control (17.5)	Industry (17)
Forgiveness (17.5)	Creativity (17.5)	Zest (18)
Gratitude (19.5)	Zest (19.5)	Spirituality (19)
Prudence (19.5)	Modesty (19.5)	Forgiveness (20)
Love of learning (21)	Love of learning (21.5)	Love of learning (21)
Modesty (22.5)	Prudence (21.5)	Prudence (22)
Beauty (22.5)	Forgiveness (23)	Modesty (23)
Spirituality (24)	Beauty (24)	Self-control (24)

Note.   RNA = Royal Norwegian Naval Academy.

Norwegians, compared to a rank of 16th for West Point cadets, who also ranked bravery much higher than did the Norwegian cadets. A thorough understanding of such differences is important to both higher echelon commanders responsible for coordinating the activities of subordinate units, and to tactical leaders who may be working together in multinational teams in operations ranging from disaster relief to full-scale warfare. It is important to note that there is no "correct" pattern of character strengths and virtues—indeed, predictive validity studies may reveal that different patterns of strengths may be equally predictive of "hard" outcome measures based on different missions and cultures. Rather, it is the difference in values and their rankings that may contribute to miscommunications and misunderstandings in multinational operations. Identifying these differences and educating forces involved in multinational operations may therefore facilitate cooperation and enhance mission effectiveness.

It is interesting to speculate about the reasons for the differences in character strengths and virtues reported here. It is not surprising that West Point cadets are higher than the U.S. civilian comparison sample on many of the traits. West Point is a selective institution, accepting fewer than 10% of applicants. To be admitted, cadets must earn high aptitude test scores, be among the best students in their high school class, and show substantial evidence of leadership potential and athletic ability. Moreover, the applicant pool consists largely of youths with a strong interest in a military career, and thus may attract applicants with a value system suited for long-term service to the nation as a commissioned officer. Thus, the finding that West Point cadets rate themselves significantly higher than the U.S. civilian comparison group on strengths such as bravery, teamwork, industry, and self-control is consistent with the sorts of values the military values and actively attempts to nurture within its own culture.[2]

Because comparable population norms on the VIA–IS are not available for Norwegian civilians, it is impossible to know where their cadets stand with respect to assessed character strengths and virtues relative to their own population. When comparing the U.S. and Norwegian cadets, the study of social axioms emerged as a promising conceptual framework for understanding and measuring cultural differences. Leung et al. (2002) proposed a five-factor structure of general beliefs or social axioms that includes the dimensions labeled cynicism, social complexity, reward for application, spirituality, and fate control. In a recent cross-cultural study, Bond et al. (2004) examined the culture-level factor structures of social axioms and its correlates across 41 nations. Interestingly, Norway and the United States were the two countries scoring lowest on the factor of societal cynicism, which could indicate a stronger sensitivity toward interpersonal relations and identification of emotions and feelings in others. On the other hand, citizens from the United States revealed higher scores than Norwegian citizens on the factor of dynamic externality, indicating stronger preferences for religious factors and individual success, which is in line with the finding in this study. In the same vein, Silvera and Seger (2004) found that Norwegians showed significantly less self-enhancement bias than did Americans, which could also be seen to reflect the perceived elite status of the West Point cadets. Taken together, recent research on cross-cultural differences seems to indicate that important variations in perceptions and information processing related to the self and general beliefs and social axioms also could be found when U.S. and Norwegian military cadets were compared on the VIA–IS. Anecdotal evidence from U.S. officers working in multinational operations suggests that these concerns are valid and warrant further empirical investigation.

Although the results reported here are intriguing, it is worth noting that making strong generalizations based on somewhat disparate samples should be done

---

[2]Because the VIA–IS was administered to the West Point cadets following their initial summer of basic cadet training, it is interesting to speculate to what extent cadets bring their values to the institution and to what extent they are developed after arriving. Although it is plausible to suggest their value patterns differ from the population prior to arrival, this is an empirical question that remains to be addressed.

with caution. The West Point sample, for example, represented volunteers who were given extra credit for participation. The Norwegian cadets, in contrast, were given the strengths survey as part of a larger testing and evaluation effort conducted by their academy and were not volunteers in the same sense as the West Point cadets. The U.S. sample consisted of persons who voluntarily logged on to a Web site and thus does not necessarily comprise a random and representative subset of the population. Future research should endeavor to utilize more consistent sampling procedures.

Ongoing research in this project is focused on establishing the criterion-based validity of character strengths and virtues. Pilot data suggest that these variables are predictive of a variety of adjustment criteria at both West Point and RNA. It is important to extend this research to other operationally significant military settings, as well as in other occupational and organizational contexts. For example, it is important to know if certain patterns of strengths and virtues are predictive of successful decision making and leadership in actual combat operations. Other areas of application are how these factors affect the ability of military personnel and their families to cope with extended separations during deployments. It may be possible to identify key character strengths and virtues important to coping skills, and to develop training interventions to reinforce and build those strengths. Finally, it is important to continue looking at how and if cultural differences in these strengths and virtues affect the ability of multinational teams to work together toward a common goal. We are also interested in comparing character strengths and virtues between West Point and civilian college students who resemble cadets in terms of aptitude and demographics, and exploring the developmental effects of Army education, training, and experience on character.

ACKNOWLEDGMENTS

The views expressed in the article are those of the authors and do not represent an official position by the U.S. Army or the Norwegian Navy.

REFERENCES

Bartone, P. T., Snook, S. A., & Tremble, T. R., Jr. (2002). Cognitive and personality predictors of leader performance in West Point Cadets. *Military Psychology, 14,* 321–338.

Bond, M. H., Leung, K., Au, A., Tong, K.-K., Carrasquel, S. R., Murakami, F., et al. (2004). Culture level dimensions of social axioms and their correlates across 41 cultures. *Journal of Cross-Cultural Psychology, 35,* 548–570.

Boring, E. G. (1950). *A history of experimental psychology* (2nd ed.). New York: Appleton-Century-Crofts.

Eid, J., Matthews, M. D., Johnsen, B. H., & Meland, N. (2005). Dispositional optimism and self-assessed situation awareness in a Norwegian military training exercise. *Perceptual and Motor Skills, 100,* 649–658.

Gibb, C. (1947). The principles and traits of leadership. *Journal of Abnormal & Social Psychology, 42,* 267–284.

Gough, H. G., Lazzari, R., Fioravanti, M., & Stracca, M. (1978). An adjective checklist scale to predict military leadership. *Journal of Cross-Cultural Psychology, 9,* 381–400.

Kelly, D. R., Matthews, M. D., & Bartone, P. T. (2005, May). *Hardiness and adaptation to a challenging military training environment.* Paper presented at the International Applied Military Psychology Symposium, Washington, DC.

Leung, K., Bond, M. H., Carrasquel, S. R., Munos, C., Hernandez, M., Murakami, F., et al. (2002). Social axioms: The search for universal dimensions of general beliefs about how the world functions. *Journal of Cross-Cultural Psychology, 33,* 286–302.

Murray, K. M., & Johnson, B. (2001). Personality type and success among female Naval Academy midshipmen. *Military Medicine, 166,* 889–893.

Peterson, C., & Seligman, M. E. P. (2004). *Character strengths and virtues: A handbook and classification.* New York: Oxford University Press.

Silvera, D. H., & Seger, C. R. (2004). Feeling good about ourselves: Unrealistic self-evaluations and their relation to self-esteem in the United States and Norway. *Journal of Cross-Cultural Psychology, 35,* 571–585.

U.S. Department of the Army. (1999). *Army leadership: Be, know, do (FM22-100).* Washington, DC: Author.

Yukl, G. (2002). *Leadership in organizations* (4th ed.). Englewood Cliffs, NJ: Prentice-Hall.

Zaccaro, S. J. (2001). *The nature of executive leadership: A conceptual and empirical analysis of success.* Washington, DC: APA Books.

MILITARY PSYCHOLOGY, 2006, *18*(Suppl.), S69–S81

Leader Development in Natural Context: A Grounded Theory Approach to Discovering How Military Leaders Grow

Gerry Larsson
Department of Leadership and Management
Swedish National Defence College
Karlstad, Sweden

Paul T. Bartone
Industrial College of the Armed Forces
National Defense University

Miepke Bos-Bakx
Royal Netherlands Military Academy
Breda, The Netherlands

Erna Danielsson
Department of Leadership and Management
Swedish National Defence College
Karlstad, Sweden

Ljubicá Jelusic
University of Ljubljana, Slovenia

Eva Johansson
Department of Leadership and Management
Swedish National Defence College
Karlstad, Sweden

Rene Moelker
Royal Netherlands Military Academy
Breda, The Netherlands

Correspondence should be addressed to Gerry Larsson, Department of Leadership and Management, Swedish National Defence College, Karolinen, SE-651 80, Karlstad, Sweden. E-mail: gerry .larsson@fhs.se

Misa Sjöberg and Aida Vrbanjac
Department of Leadership and Management
Swedish National Defence College
Karlstad, Sweden

Jocelyn Bartone
Davidsonville, Maryland

George B. Forsythe
U.S. Military Academy

Andreas Pruefert
EUROMIL—European Organization of Military Associations
Brussels, Belgium

Mariusz Wachowicz
Military Bureau for Sociological Research
Polish Defense Ministry
Warsaw, Poland

Despite an increasing number of programs that aim to develop or educate leaders, the underlying processes involved in leader development or growth are not well understood. This study was undertaken to discover what factors or processes are involved in leader development for junior military officers, from their own perspective and in the natural context of their career and life experiences. Military officers ($N = 51$) from 5 different countries were interviewed using a standardized approach, and interview transcripts were analyzed according to the constant comparative method of grounded theory, as elaborated by Glaser and Strauss (1967). Consistently across the 5 countries, the core of the process model of leader development is the social interaction between the young officer and his or her significant others (soldiers, peers, and superiors). In the favorable case, officers end this process feeling secure, being able to flexibly adapt their overt behavior on an underdistanced–overdistanced continuum according to situational demands, and have a firm professional identity.

Military organizations have historically placed great emphasis on the value of good leadership, and have sought in various ways to train or develop effective leaders. For military organizations today, the fact of broadening roles and missions also puts additional demands on military leaders (Moskos, Williams, & Segal, 2000), making leadership an even more important concern for military organizations. This has led to a recent increase in attention to the question of what skills, attributes, or competencies military leaders might need to be effective in this new, more complex environment (e.g., Caforio, 2001; Snider & Watkins, 2002). Among factors considered are flexibility, cultural awareness, cognitive complexity, openness, broad perspective, and tolerance for ambiguity. Still, the focus has mainly been on end-state leader qualities. The underlying developmental processes through which people grow or develop into different and better leaders are poorly understood, and remain relatively unexamined.

Of course, interest in leadership is not limited to military organizations. Quite a vast literature exists on leadership, including empirical, theoretical, and anecdotal attempts to understand what qualities make for a good leader (Bass, 1990, 1998; Burns, 1978; House & Howell, 1992). Also, extensive attention has been devoted to training programs and practices aimed at enhancing leadership skills and capabilities (see, e.g., Avolio, 1999, 2005; McCauley, Moxley, & Van Velsor, 1998). Such programs include various feedback strategies, mentoring, executive coaching, and skills-development workshops (e.g., McDonald-Mann, 1998). However, as Day (2001) pointed out in a recent review, leader development practice is mostly disconnected from any scientific foundation, and as regards leadership development, there is a "relative dearth of scholarly research directly on the topic" (p. 582).[1] Research and theory generation are sorely needed in this area.

This study directly addresses the question of what factors influence the development of good leaders in the military, and seeks to clarify what the natural developmental process itself might entail. In the interest of developing new ideas and theory about leader development, we undertook a cross-national grounded theory (Glaser & Strauss, 1967) qualitative study of leader development in junior military officers in five different countries. Studies such as this one address the theory-generating aspect of the scientific enterprise, as opposed to theory testing or evaluation. Thus we are not concerned with hypothesis testing, but rather with generating new ideas and hypotheses for future evaluation. As elaborated by Glaser and Strauss (1967) and Strauss and Corbin (1998), grounded theory describes theoretical formulations that are closely grounded in raw data, usually text of some form. The grounded theory approach requires investigators to approach their data without preconceived ideas, theories, or hypotheses about what they will find. Rather, through rigorous and detailed iterative analyses, theory emerges more or less directly from the data.

METHOD

Informants

The study was carried out in five countries: The Netherlands, Norway, Slovenia, Sweden, and the United States.[2] Ten military officers were interviewed in each

---

[1]See also Zaccaro (2001) for an excellent review of leadership theory and research, focusing on the executive or "strategic" level of leadership.

[2]Although not included in this report, leader development interviews were also conducted in Canada (Sarah Hill), Italy (Roberto Chiabert), and the Czech Republic (Jitka Laštovková).

country. Following the guidelines of grounded theory (Glaser & Strauss, 1967), the selection of participants was guided by a desire to find informants with a wide variety of experiences. The actual selection process however, could probably best be described as a combination of this ideal and practical convenience (e.g., availability of participants). Demographic and basic military data for the whole group of informants are shown in Table 1.

Data Collection

Data were collected using semistructured interviews, following a prepared interview guide. The interviews consisted of open-ended questions and individually adapted follow-up questions. Participants were asked to report on their military experiences since being commissioned, and to discuss any experiences or events that they recalled as particularly important or developmental for them as leaders. Follow-up questions focused on the following areas:

- Experiences and career milestones.
- Officer development and training.
- Strengths and weaknesses (own leadership).
- Contribution to effectiveness and satisfaction.

The interviews all took place between March 2004 and April 2005 at the informants' working places. Interviews were audio recorded, and lasted from 60 to 120 min. An effort was made to calibrate interview styles at a work group meeting prior to commencing the research. All interviews were conducted and analyzed by the authors.

TABLE 1
Demographic Data From Cross-National Samples

Country	Gender		Married/ Cohabit		Age in Years		Rank (Range)	Service Experience in Years		Service
	Male	Female	Yes	No	M	Range		M	Range	
The Netherlands	8	2	7	3	27.8	26–31	1Lt–Cpt	5	3–6	Army/Air Force
Norway	4	6	7	3	30.3	26–37	Lt Cdr–Cdr	10.5	4.5–15	Navy
Slovenia	10	1	8	3	36.4	27–47	2Lt–LtCol	11.9	6–17	Army
Sweden	9	1	6	4	26.0	23–29	1Lt–2Lt	3.1	1.5–5	Army/Air Force
United States	8	2	9	1	31.7	29–35	Cpt–Major	9.1	7–11	Army
Total sample	39	12	37	14	30.5	23–47	2Lt–LtCol	8	1.5–17	

Note. 1Lt = first lieutenant; Cpt = captain; Lt Cdr = lieutenant commander; Cdr = commander; 2Lt = second lieutenant; LtCol = lieutenant colonel.

Data Analysis

The interviews were transcribed verbatim and analyzed according to the constant comparative method introduced by Glaser and Strauss (1967). These authors described this method as consisting of the following four stages:

> (1) comparing incidents applicable to each category, (2) integrating categories and their properties, (3) delimiting the theory, and (4) writing the theory. Although this method of generating theory is a continuously growing process—each stage after a time being transformed into the next—earlier stages do remain in operation simultaneously throughout the analysis and each provides continuous development to its successive stage until the analysis is terminated. (p. 105)

This was done independently within each country data set, first identifying the most elemental meaning units, and then grouping these together into categories and subcategories, properties, and unifying concepts.

The first step in this analytic procedure is described as open coding. Data were examined line by line to identify the informants' descriptions of thought patterns, feelings, and actions related to leader development mentioned in the interviews. The codes derived were formulated in words resembling those used by the informants. For example, the statement "I've asked the soldiers for feedback, positive and negative on everything. I received a lot of written feedback that I've never thought of. A lot of feedback to reflect over" was coded as "getting feedback." Codes were then compared to verify their descriptive content and to confirm they were well grounded in the data. This was done independently by the researchers from each country following a practice session at a work group meeting.

In the second step of analysis, the codes were translated into English and sorted into different categories. To illustrate, the preceding example, getting feedback, was sorted into the somewhat broader category "everyday interaction in military schools and national regiments." This was done by making constant comparisons between interview protocols, codes, and categories (Glaser & Strauss, 1967; Strauss & Corbin, 1998). Codes and categories were also analyzed with respect to the somewhat different military roles and structures found across the participating countries. This step, as well as the next, was performed in collaboration at a work group meeting.

The third step consisted of fitting together all categories using the constant comparative method. In practice, the steps of analysis were not strictly sequential. Rather, we proceeded iteratively backward and forward, constantly reexamining interview data, codes, and categories. This resulted in a hypothesized process model of leader development in young military officers.

RESULTS

In this section the whole model is presented first, followed by a presentation of its categories and some quotations. This order of presentation provides greater clarity regarding the meaning of the parts in relation to the whole model.

The idea of process is inherent in the development concept. Although developmental outcomes or end states are certainly important, here we are most interested in understanding the processes by which young officers change or grow. With this in mind, the presentation of a model of leader development in young military officers will be process oriented. It begins with a starting position, followed by two qualitatively different process descriptions, and ends with a resulting position. The presentation has an ideal typical character; real-world issues such as individual differences are left out to gain clarity.

The core of the process model of leader development is the everyday social interaction between the young officer and his or her significant others (soldiers, peers, and superiors). This interaction takes place in particular organizational contexts (e.g., a military school, a national regiment, or an international mission), which, in turn, are part of a broader national and cultural context. The young officer enters this system with his or her personal resources (e.g., physical strength, personality, earlier leadership experiences, education and training, etc.). Thus, in metatheoretical terms, the model rests on a person-by-situation interactional paradigm (Endler & Magnusson, 1976).

Starting Position

Typical story line.   The young officer has little formal power and lacks inner security. He or she may seek to compensate for this by publicly behaving in an overdistanced way toward the soldiers. The professional identity as a military officer is weak. In contrast, significant superior role models are perceived as having formal power, being secure and able to flexibly adapt their overt behavior on an underdistanced–overdistanced continuum according to situational demands, and to have a firm professional identity. In summary, a gap exists between the young officer and his or her significant role models in all these respects.

Narrative illustration.   When looking back on the early phases of their professional careers as military officers, several participants gave responses that reflected an inner insecurity. To illustrate:

> I was a student in the school, I did not consider myself a leader. I wasn't the stick [group] leader, I was just there as a student.

> I struggled through airborne school, I was terrified. So that the whole time there was just a nightmare for me.

How I viewed myself. I did not view myself as a leader, and when I realized or when it was pointed out to me that my actions impacted others then it really had a significant meaning.

You'll be confronted with a whole different kind of personnel. Then you think you are, and you will discover that, the leader you were at the Royal Military Academy doesn't fit at all anymore.

Setting the right example was also emphasized, as is nicely illustrated in the following excerpt:

And it was more I realized that as a LT that sometimes you come in late or you may be like, "Well, I don't need to be there right now, the soldiers don't need to see me. I can do this. I've some errands to run." It was, "I'm going to be down there. I'm going to be the first guy in every day. I've got to set the example." And it was just a significant event where you know I realized how hard or how, how important discipline is and setting the example as a leader was.

Obviously, not all responses indicated an inner weakness. The following two citations illustrate strong confidence and gradual learning, respectively.

Well, I've been a leader since I was very young, a scout leader, and I have had judo groups and things like that.

And I realized then that ... I have not only the skills to guide the ship but the ability to prioritize, and decide what needed to be done first and what needed to be done second. It was overwhelming, the job, at times, but everything got done ... I reached that point gradually through ... working with other people. That was a very useful thing to make, that experience and that realization later on in situations that were equally delicate or more so, and I could say, you know, I can prove myself, I'm able to do this.

Process Description 1: The Educational and National Regiment Context

Typical story line. At the core of the everyday interaction in military schools and national training regiments are, from the perspective of the young officer, seeing significant role models (superiors and peers) do something, then doing it themselves, and then getting feedback. It is assumed that the overt behavior toward subordinates will gradually become more flexibly distanced, and the inner security and the sense of a professional identity will grow. The significant others at all levels will respond positively to this. Similarly, if the young officer does not proceed with the socialization process along this path, the significant others will respond negatively, and the individual will experience social anxiety. Events contributing to the process are promotion in rank (more formal power), successful role transitions (sometimes planned, sometimes random), and being part of a military culture and way of life also when off duty. Compared to the situation at the onset, the young officer has moved his position in a favorable direction on all these characteristics.

Narrative illustration.   Some factors contributing to leader development—positively or negatively—appear to be common across all studied nations. The importance of role models is an example. The following two excerpts from the interviews illustrate both the positive and negative impact of role models.

> I have several role models at my company, for example, my captain. He does a lot of good things I try to copy in my leadership. So my colleagues are my role models, even those I have studied together with. You see them do good stuff, and then you try to do the same. My captain for example, before he solves a problem, he sits down and analyzes it first, instead of just doing something directly. So I have learned to calm down, and think for a while, before I do something.

> When you're in the training system and you know, your officer is supposed to be exemplary and ... there he is in the troop office, and he's got his feet up on the warrant's desk, he's picking his nose and you're standing right in front of him, and he's cursing and swearing, and talking about some girl he picked up in the bar, in front of you, and the guy can barely do 25 push-ups, like that is just not the type of behavior I would expect from someone who is in charge of me.

Another common theme was the impact of realistic and challenging exercises. In the words of one of our informants:

> Both the leadership exercises and the winter exercise—where I learned how to handle and lead people in different situations. That's absolutely something I've had use for later. Those exercises made me see both myself and others that I perhaps had an idea of. For my own sake, just to learn that you can take on so unbelievably much more that you think. How strong you get, even when you feel that you've reached bottom there is incredibly much more left to give.

Some contributions were more specific to a given military context. A couple of new illustrations:

> Pregnancy and childbirth forces one to shore duty [gender-specific rule for female Norwegian officers].

> Our system forces all officers to start at the bottom [Swedish system with no noncommissioned officers].

> I also experienced that there is a difference between civilian and military employees. Soldiers accept your rank, where you come from. So that was much easier than the ci-

vilian approach [officer from the Netherlands on differences between the civilian and the military culture].

Process Description 2: The Real-World (Sharp) Military Mission Context

Typical story line.   Despite the favorable development process previously described, there is an important thing lacking in the professional officer identity. This reflects a difference between military officers and, possibly, all other professional groups. A physician, for example, begins to treat real patients after leaving medical school. The situation for military officers is different. After leaving the military academy, they tend to work in a teacher role at national military regiments. The problem with this, from a professional identity perspective, is that they are not tested in the very core activity of their profession: the real-world or "sharp" military mission. Thus, it is only after the completion of one or more such missions that the leader development process moves to a qualitatively higher level. Typical comments were "I finally got a receipt" and "Now I know I can handle the stress of military leadership." A confirmation of the professional identity—positive or negative depending on how they responded to the leader role during a mission—takes place.

Narrative illustration.   We illustrate this aspect of leader development with five interview excerpts that all seem to capture a common experience among the informants.

> The war experience, where I had to command the reservists without enough knowledge, led to my increasing motivation for military education. Now I feel more knowledgeable and better prepared for the job, although war has left an important experience in me: I changed my relation towards the subordinates, now I respect them more, I listen to them, because I understand how much I am (I was in war) responsible for all of them and to all of them and their families. I value life much higher than before the war.

> The biggest impact on my leadership development had a stressful situation in 1991, in war for independent Slovenia [June–July 1991]. I worked as officer in Territorial Army Command in one local community. When it came to war, I realized that I don't have enough knowledge on real use of units in battles. I did not have any practical experience, the circumstances were very specific, and in reality all theories of force deployment were not useful. I would need practical experiences, which Territorial Army of that time did not have. I also found out that the meaning of life in war is totally different from what we know in peace. My conclusion was that for every individual leader in the military the permanent education and self-education are of utmost importance. We also must learn from other militaries that are involved in wars or finished wars recently. Otherwise all wars would come as full surprise.

I think that second most important impact on my understanding of leadership had the participation in peace operation KFOR in 2002, where I was staff officer in International Headquarters. I learned that good leaders must very quickly adapt to changed circumstances (previous experiences and personal characteristics helped me to adapt). I met new procedures and work in that international staff, but I also realized that my army, Slovenian army, is comparable to other European armies. I felt a lack of knowledge of military work in an international environment. I developed a higher level of tolerance and realized how important is to know foreign languages in a military job. I learned that a military officer in the 21st century has to adapt to different roles, because an officer has to switch from officer manager to officer-negotiator, he or she must be able to make compromises and to be tolerant toward other militaries. If I would have some more chances to go on peace missions or international exercises, I would develop my military leadership skills much better. As a female officer I had to show more experience and expertise in the role of commander. A good leader must understand himself or herself well, must be able to make decisions, must listen, and must have expertise.

I have noticed a difference in my own attitude when I came home from the peacekeeping mission. I've seen what we are educated for, and that was the hardest point before I went. To motivate the soldiers for something I had no idea of why we were doing, but now I know, and I can stand up for it. Today I educate the soldiers in a different way. For example, I don't think it's so important to know what a mine weighs, but it's important that the soldiers can handle it.

I have the feeling that I can't be a good commander because of lack of mission experience. I feel my colleagues are thinking in that way about me. Right now I'm not in the position to go abroad, but when the children are older, I will go for the experience.

Resulting Theoretical Position

Typical story line.   In the favorable case, the process described earlier implies that, after a few years, the young officer has developed into the position his or her significant superior role models had at the onset (at least according to the perception of the beginning officer). Now he or she has more formal power, the inner world is more secure, the overt behavior is flexible, and the professional identity as a military officer is well established.

DISCUSSION

Leader development in young military officers appears to entail two cooccurring processes. One is inner or private, and is characterized by a gradual strengthening of the feeling of security. The other is overt or public, and consists of a gradual change from overdistanced behavior toward subordinates to a flexible adaptation

along an underdistanced–overdistanced continuum according to situational demands. Two main determinants of these processes were identified. First, the everyday social interaction between the young officer and his or her significant others
(soldiers, peers, and superiors) is crucial. Observing role models and getting feedback were mentioned as important sources of influence in all countries. Second,
taking part in real-world military missions strongly contributes to a confirmation
of the officer's professional identity.

Interestingly, planned leadership development courses, for instance, including
group dynamic exercises, were hardly mentioned at all by the informants. This
could be due to the interview scheme—this kind of training was not directly addressed. It could also be due to having negative experiences from such exercises.
However, we believe the main reason is that it reflects the importance ascribed to
the day-in, day-out experience of social interaction and natural group dynamics.
This interpretation is consistent with the findings of Packard (1999), who observed
leader development in U.S. Air Force cadets over a 4-year period.

The leader development process could also be interpreted from a work socialization perspective. In the typical military officer case, it appears that learning and
actual work are closely intertwined. This is consistent with social constructivist
writings (e.g., Berger & Luckman, 1966; Lave & Wenger, 1991; Weibull, 2003)
and fits in a broader symbolic interactionistic paradigm.

According to our interpretation of the interviews, there is, however, one important part missing in this theoretical perspective on leader development. For the military officer, entering military schools and learning on the job after these schools is
not enough. The core of the professional identity is not confirmed until he or she
has experienced one or more real-world (sharp) military missions. The different
stressors in such missions and the way they are appraised and coped with make significant contributions to the individual leader development process. This finding
appears to fit nicely with the psychological stress theoretical model of Lazarus
(1991, 1999).

Our findings emphasizing a process of interaction between the individual and
the social and organizational environment also support Day's (2001) argument that
leader development involves not just individual-level considerations; it is a more
complex phenomenon that necessarily entails an interaction of the individual with
the organizational environment. Indeed, our view of the leader development process, based on these multinational data, would seem to bridge what Day described
as the individual–human capital concept of leader development, and the more rela-
tional–social capital concept of leadership development.

Obviously, in reality there are a number of potential deviations from the favorable ideal typical development process just described. Principally, the sources of
these can be found within the individual, in the situational context, and in the person–situation interaction of a particular case. Examples of individual-related
sources of deviations include inadequate physical or psychological resources,

problems outside the professional life, and so forth. Examples of context-related sources of deviations are poor role models, being placed in a subculture one finds ethically and morally unacceptable, lack of missions or missions that are impossible to solve even for the best, and so on. In the favorable case, the young officer ends up with fulfilled expectations, whereas in the unfavorable case the expectations are unrealized or disrupted by a reality that is dramatically different from that anticipated.

In constructing our current model we were limited to data obtained from a selected group of military officers. It should also be emphasized that the concepts derived from the data may be of a sensitizing rather than a definitive character in Blumer's (1954) words. Bringing a variety of leadership actions together under a heading such as "seeing significant role models do" could, for example, be questioned, although these actual words occurred frequently in the interviews. It should also be noted that the study relies on self-reported data only. These may be inaccurate, and a broader range of data would have been desirable. Little is also currently known about the generalizability of the model. However, this was not the goal of this qualitative study. In the general terms of Glaser and Strauss (1967), "Partial testing of theory, when necessary, is left to more rigorous approaches (sometimes qualitative but usually quantitative). These come later in the scientific enterprise" (p. 103). Thus, further studies are needed of leader development in a variety of contexts to develop, formalize, and evaluate the utility of this model.

REFERENCES

Avolio, B. J. (1999). *Full leadership development: Building the vital forces in organizations.* Thousand Oaks, CA: Sage.

Avolio, B. J. (2005). *Leadership development in balance: Made/born.* Mahwah, NJ: Lawrence Erlbaum Associates, Inc.

Bass, B. M. (1990). *Bass & Stogdill's handbook of leadership* (3rd ed.). New York: The Free Press.

Bass, B. M. (1998). *Transformational leadership.* Mahwah, NJ: Lawrence Erlbaum Associates, Inc.

Berger, P., & Luckman, R. (1966). *The social construction of reality: A treatise in the sociology of logics.* London: Penguin.

Blumer, H. (1954). What is wrong with social research. *American Sociological Review, 14,* 3–10.

Burns, J. M. (1978). *Leadership.* New York: Harper & Row.

Caforio, G. (Ed.). (2001). *The flexible officer.* Rome: Artistic & Publishing Company.

Day, D. V. (2001). Leadership development: A review in context. *Leadership Quarterly, 11,* 581–613.

Endler, N. S., & Magnusson, D. (1976). Toward an interactional psychology of personality. *Psychology Bulletin, 83,* 956–974.

Glaser, B., & Strauss, A. (1967). *The discovery of grounded theory: Strategies for qualitative research.* New York: Aldine.

House, R. J., & Howell, J. M. (1992). Personality and charismatic leadership. *Leadership Quarterly, 3,* 81–108.

Lave, W., & Wenger, E. (1991). *Situated learning: Legitimate peripheral participation.* Cambridge, England: Cambridge University Press.

Lazarus, R. S. (1991). *Emotion and adaptation.* New York: Oxford University Press.

Lazarus, R. S. (1999). *Stress and emotion: A new synthesis.* London: Free Association Books.

McCauley, C. D., Moxley, R. S., & Van Velsor, E. (Eds.). (1998). *Handbook of leadership development.* San Francisco: Jossey-Bass.

McDonald-Mann, D. G. (1998). Skill-based training. In C. D. McCauley, R. S. Moxley, & E. Van Velsor (Eds.), *Handbook of leadership development* (pp. 106–126). San Francisco: Jossey-Bass.

Moskos, C. C., Williams, J. A., & Segal, D. R. (2000). *The postmodern military: Armed forces after the Cold War.* New York: Oxford University Press.

Packard, G. A. (1999). *Longitudinal study of the social network influences on the leadership and military development of cadets at the U.S. Air Force Academy.* Chapel Hill: University of North Carolina.

Snider, D. M., & Watkins, G. L. (Eds.). (2002). *The future of the Army profession.* New York: McGraw-Hill Primis.

Strauss, A., & Corbin, J. (1998). *Basics of qualitative research: Techniques and procedures for developing grounded theory.* Thousand Oaks, CA: Sage.

Weibull, A. (2003). Att utvecklas som ledare: Organisationsnivå [To develop as leader: Organizational level]. In G. Larsson & K. Kallenberg (Eds.), *Direkt ledarskap* (pp. 296–309). Stockholm, Sweden: Försvarsmakten.

Zaccaro, S. J. (2001). *The nature of executive leadership.* Washington, DC: American Psychological Association.

MILITARY PSYCHOLOGY, 2006, *18*(Suppl.), S83–S101
Copyright © 2006, Lawrence Erlbaum Associates, Inc.

Raising the Flag: Promotion to Admiral in the United States Navy

David A. Schwind
U.S. Naval Academy

Janice H. Laurence
Office of the Under Secretary of Defense
U.S. Department of Defense

A qualitative analysis of the salient considerations for selection to Rear Admiral (Lower Half) in the United States Navy was conducted. Semistructured interviews were conducted with 18 active-duty and retired flag officers. Overall, reputation and fitness report rankings were reported to be important factors in the promotion of flag officers. Contrary to expectations, commissioning source and letters of recommendation were reported to be not heavily weighted.

Throughout seafaring history, commanding officers of a squadron or fleet (consisting of any two or more vessels) have traditionally been known as *flag officers*. This moniker stems from flying an identifying command pennant or flag atop a flagship (Reynolds, 2002). In the U.S. Navy today, flag officers refer to its admirals or those in the top officer pay grades (i.e., O7 to O10). As of 2003, there were 224 flag officers on active duty, constituting only 0.4% of all active-duty officers. Approximately 50% of flag officers are O7s (rear admiral, lower half), about 35% are O8s (rear admiral, upper half), and approximately 15% make up the top two pay grades, O9 (vice admiral) and O10 (admiral).

The Navy officer corps consists of two divisions: restricted (RL) and unrestricted line (URL) officers. The RL includes medical corps, dental corps, and other officers who are ineligible for command at sea. The majority of flag officers are URL. These command-eligible surface warfare officers (SWO), pilots, naval flight officers (NFO), and submariners are the focus of this study.

Correspondence should be addressed to Janice H. Laurence, Office of the Under Secretary of Defense, Personnel & Readiness, Pentagon, Room 3C980, Washington, DC 20301–4000. E-mail: janice.laurence@osd.mil

For URL officers, there are three primary commissioning sources: the U.S. Naval Academy (USNA), Naval Reserve Officer Training Corps (NROTC), and Officer Candidate School (OCS). Promotion rates to flag rank vary greatly among commissioning sources. The senior ranks of the Navy tend to be filled disproportionately by USNA alumni (Bowman, 1991; Eitelberg, Laurence, & Brown, 1992; Janowitz, 1971; Moore & Trout, 1978; Woelper, 1998).

Visibility is one explanation for the continued success of USNA graduates (Moore & Trout, 1978). Four years at the USNA, in a Navy environment, gives graduates a higher level of experience and greater adaptability to life in the fleet than junior officers from other commissioning sources (Moore & Trout, 1978). Bowman (1991) noted that the relatively high percentage of USNA graduates in senior ranks particularly in the aviation and surface warfare communities, may be attributed to the greater inclination for USNA graduates to remain in the Navy, and the increased chances of graduates to be selected for promotion. The higher retention and promotion rates among USNA alumni may stem from self-selection; a graduate may expect a career in the Navy even before entering the USNA (Woelper, 1998).

In addition to commissioning source, community and assignments within community factor into promotion to flag. Certainly, performance is also a key. Better officers with more competitive records are typically assigned to more career-enhancing jobs, allowing them to achieve further career milestones. In addition, graduate education is also career enhancing. However, although the Navy's senior leadership has stated its desire for officers to obtain graduate education, some officers (and some officer communities) still believe that the time away from the fleet while earning a graduate degree makes them less competitive for future promotion (Buterbaugh, 1995).

Research on the effects of graduate education at the flag officer levels is sparse. Multiple studies have concluded that graduate education has a limited positive effect on promotion at the O3 through O6 pay grades, depending on warfare specialty. Among all officers (RL and URL) at the O4 through O7 promotion levels, Cymrot (1986) found that graduate education had a positive effect on promotion up to selection to flag rank. In a more recent study, Buterbaugh (1995) found that graduate education was a positive factor in promotions to the O5 and O6 pay grades in some warfare designators. At the O6 level, graduate education was significant only in the surface warfare community. It had a negative effect in the submarine, pilot, and NFO communities.

Bowman and Mehay (1999) studied the effects of graduate education in the promotion of officers to the O4 pay grade and found that promotion probabilities were 10 to 15 points higher for those officers having any graduate degree. Further, those officers who completed their graduate education through one of the Navy's fully funded, full-time programs increased their chances of promotion to O4 by 15 to 17 points over an officer without a graduate degree. A caveat, however, is that officers who participate in these graduate programs often have additional unobserved attributes that may make them more promotable, even without the added benefit of graduate education.

The Goldwater–Nichols Defense Reorganization Act of 1986 was created to improve the war-fighting capability of the United States by ending service parochialism. The Act included provisions that required joint professional military education (JPME) to prepare officers for joint duty. Additionally, the Act included that a joint duty assignment be a prerequisite for promotion to flag officer (Savage, 1992). In the past, good-of-the-service waivers have been granted routinely to selected flag officers not having joint experience prior to their flag-rank promotion. These officers have primarily been from the aviation and submarine communities, as their career timelines often did not allow for such an assignment.

For advancement in the Navy, Walsh (1997) described the need for progressively responsible leadership positions as well as postgraduate and JPME, joint duty assignments and tours in Washington, DC, and at service headquarters, in addition to operational tours. Early assignments are expected to develop the officer as an expert in a warfare specialty. They build functional skills, general organizational knowledge, and personal insight (Brancato, Harrell, Schirmer, & Thie, 2004). The later tours test the acquired skills in more complex and often ambiguous assignments (Brancato et al., 2004). The skills and competencies developed in these jobs, the personal networks formed, and the reputation an officer establishes become the next step in the dynamics of an officer's promotion to flag rank. However, there is more to selection to flag rank than completing graduate and joint education, a successful command at sea, or a Washington or joint headquarters job.

A 1982 study of 15 successful general managers from a broad cross-section of U.S. businesses (Kotter, 1982) noted the following chain of events: (a) the manager did well in an early assignment; (b) this success led to a promotion or more challenging assignment; (c) successful performance and recognition positively influenced self-esteem, motivation, and effectiveness and led to additional opportunities that likewise built additional skills; (d) relevant relationships developed (including mentoring by top management), enhancing interpersonal and intellectual skills; and (e) these newly acquired skills and relationships led to higher performance in the next, more challenging job, thus perpetuating the pattern. In sum, reputation, work-related competencies, and the building of interpersonal relationships influence future promotions.

As an officer moves up through the ranks, performance becomes more difficult to measure. Additionally, by the time an officer reaches the senior levels, the promotion process has (normally) prevented substandard performers from attaining higher rank, and thus, all performance evaluations at this level tend to be stellar. The distinguishing factor among officers at this career point is visibility. An officer achieves a reputation by serving successfully in a high-visibility job.

This serves to establish a network of relationships (Moore & Trout, 1978). What develops is a self-fulfilling prophecy, wherein officers who have proven themselves are not only expected to do well, but are often assigned future jobs based on this expectation. In short, "early high-visibility billets lead to subsequent high-visibility billets" (Moore & Trout, 1978, p. 462). Later, the actual impact of performance lessens as an officer rises in seniority and the visibility factor increases dramatically, largely determining the future assignment of an officer. By this point a pattern of superior performance has already formed, and the visible officer, based on his or her reputation, has been assigned to more elite and higher level jobs working for officers who are themselves outstanding (Moore & Trout, 1978).

The final ingredients crucial for flag rank selection are competencies. Because flag officers are expected to be able to capably operate outside their warfare specialty, other skills and competencies are valued. In the civilian world, behavioral competencies noted as being vital to executive success include interpersonal skills, leadership skills, business management skills, and personal attributes (Byham, Paese, & Smith, 2002).

The Navy's career framework is built on the concept that work experience in various assignments prepares a person for more challenging and complex future jobs (Brancato et al., 2004). Jobs held early in a career tend to build functional skills and general organizational knowledge. Later assignments tend to have more complex and ambiguous aspects, requiring the application of much of the organizational knowledge and skills learned in the past, and the building of secondary skills or competencies (Brancato et al., 2004).

Personnel selection, assessment, assignment, training, development, and leadership are among the key arenas in which psychological study and applications have benefitted the military. However, understanding the personnel characteristics, traits, performance dimensions, and other behaviors associated with the military's executives has escaped open scrutiny and documentation. This qualitative study begins to fill this void with a rare glimpse at the process and factors considered for promotion to flag rank or admiral in the Navy.

METHOD

Archival data from the records of 100 out of a possible 108 URL flag officers belonging to year groups (YGs) 1972 through 1978[1] were examined for commonalities or patterns in career experiences and background variables. Together with the literature review findings, the archival data led to the development of a protocol to

---

[1]YG is the classification of all officers commissioned during a fiscal year. For example, officers commissioned between October 1, 1972 and September 30, 1973 are considered part of YG 1973.

be used for interviewing flag officer promotion experts. That is, semistructured interviews were conducted with former members of O7 selection boards from fiscal year (FY) 1994 through 1999. Additional flag officers were interviewed, including a former chief of naval operations and chiefs and deputy chiefs of naval personnel, because of their unique perspectives.

Archival Data

Official Navy biographies of the active-duty flag officers from the YGs in the sample were obtained from the official Navy Web site[2] or, for those that were incomplete or not so posted, on request from the flag officers. In total, information from 100 complete biographies was obtained. Biography data were verified and supplemented by data from the Navy's Officer Master File (OMF) obtained from the Defense Manpower Data Center (DMDC) regarding commissioning source, education, and career history.

Qualitative Data

Interviews with a convenience sample of 18 retired and active-duty flag officers were conducted. Only officers who had either been part of a flag officer selection board or had accumulated considerable experience in flag and senior officer promotions were deemed eligible for interview. From the 49 retired members from the O7 promotion boards dating from FYs 1994, 1996, 1998, and 1999, a convenience sample of 23 was identified as flag officers residing within traveling distance. Of this group, 9 admirals were willing to be interviewed. To bolster the sample, an interview request was sent to the remaining 26 officers; 9 additional flag officers agreed to be interviewed. Thus, the resulting sample of 18 was less of a convenience sample than originally planned. Table 1 provides background information for each of the flag officers interviewed.

After providing a preview of the protocol, in-person, semistructured interviews[3] were conducted on a nonattribution basis by the first author (a Navy lieutenant) in conjunction with his thesis required in partial fulfillment for the Master of Science in Leadership and Human Resource Development from the Naval Postgraduate School. (The second author served as primary thesis advisor.) The interviews lasted between 40 min and 155 min, with an average of 90 min, during which time 12 questions were posed. The questions were derived from the findings in the literature and archival data regarding factors hypothesized to be related to promotion. All but three interviews were audio recorded. Recordings were made with the interviewee's direct consent. The data were content ana-

---

[2]See http://www.chinfo.navy.mil/navpalib/people/flags/biographies/bios-top.html.
[3]One interview was conducted over the phone because of scheduling conflicts.

TABLE 1
Biographical Information for Flag Officer Sample Members

Admiral	Warfare Specialty	O7 Boards	Commissioning Source	Rank	Retirement Year
A	Sub	4	USNA	O8	2000
B	SWO	2	USNA	O8	2000
C	Sub	2	USNA	O10	1990
D	Aviation	0	USNA	O9	1986
E	SWO	0	ROTC	O8	2001
F	Aviation	4	USNA	O8	1998
G	SWO	1	ROTC	O9	1997
H	Aviation	5	USNA	O10	2000
I	SWO	7	USNA	O8	2003
J	SWO	2	ROTC	O9	2000
K	Aviation	1	USNA	O9	2002
L	SWO	0	ROTC	O8	1997
M	Fleet Sup	8	OCS	O8	1998
N	Sub	2	USNA	O9	1998
O	Sub	3	USNA	O8	1998
P	SWO	0	USNA	O9	NA
Q	Aviation	2	OCS	O7	2000
R	Sub	2	ROTC	O8	1995

Note.   Sub = submarine; SWO = surface warfare officer; Fleet Sup = fleet support; USNA = U.S. Naval Academy; ROTC = Reserve Officer Training Corps; OCS = Officer Candidate School; NA = not available.

lyzed with major categories identified. A line-by-line review of transcripts made from the audio recordings was conducted and themes were identified corresponding to the topics posed to the respondents. The data were analyzed in this manner by the first author and reviewed by the second author. Note that in describing the results and providing exemplary quotes, masculine pronouns are the norm. This is influenced by the underrepresentation of women especially at high levels in the military and the restriction to male flag officer nominees in the sample used to examine career trends.

RESULTS

Selection Board Process

Before describing the characteristics of flag nominees considered, views of the interviewees regarding the selection board process are presented. The O7 URL selection board is composed of 15 to 18 flag officers typically in pay grades O7 and O8, representing each URL community. Three flag officers in the O9 pay grade are also included on the board to be the senior representatives of their respective communities. Finally, one O10 presides as board president, setting the direction and tone of the selection board and ensuring the fulfillment of the board precept. Although the president of the board is very influential, he has only one vote.

The board is highly regulated by statutory law, and the members of the board take their direction from the precept, or formal guidance from the Secretary of the Navy, as to what skills the Navy needs in its future flag officers. The precept for a statutory board gives both general and specific guidance regarding the criteria on which board selection should be made. During the interviews, every one of the admirals noted how the board ran by the letter of the precept. As Admiral J, a former Deputy Chief of Naval Personnel (DCNP), put it:

> In my experience, the presidents of these boards read, and reread, and reread precepts. The Secretary of the Navy signs these things. It is "The Word." And so the most important things about that selection board are determined by what the Secretary chose to say in the precept. If the Secretary says: "Read my lips: I want solid joint experience. I am looking for people that served on joint staffs, served in operational joint assignments, at the war fighting commands." Whatever it is that the Secretary says the board really cues to that guidance. They realize their statutory responsibility.

All records that come up for consideration for promotion to O7 are divided among the members of the selection board for review. The records contain Fitness Reports (FITREPs), records of tours experienced, graduate school information, any adverse documentation, and more. Each board member briefs the records assigned. The briefer primarily serves as an advocate for the officer whom the record represents, but also has the responsibility to note any adverse items. Most important, the briefer must frame the record in the context of the needs of the Navy, as delineated by the precept.

Board members represent all URL communities, thus a member of one community may brief the record of an officer from another community, such as a submariner briefing the record of a pilot. Because of variations in briefing skills, each record is briefed by two officers. The interviewees all agreed that the briefer had little impact on the final outcome of the selection board. Even though some briefers may be better than others, the interviewees agreed that if the candidate had a good record, it would be noted, no matter the quality of the briefer. Admiral I noted:

> Usually, the people in the room who look at your record look at the totality of your record and how you do as a Captain. Whether the briefer is a fumble-fingered-mumble-mouse or he is Abraham Lincoln, the record is the record. So, if you've got a bad record, I don't care who you are, it's just not going to make it.

In the more senior ranks, it is certainly possible that the person briefing a record personally knows, or at least knows of, the officer being briefed. This knowledge can be a significant help or hindrance to a candidate. The overwhelming opinion of the interviewees was that voiced high regard by a briefer had a great impact in the decision of the board members. Conversely, if a member of the board knew a candidate, and either did not discuss him in glowing terms or consciously refrained from discussing him, a negative message was conveyed to the other members of the board.[4] However, having personal knowledge of a candidate did not guarantee his promotion. Admiral B stated:

> If you have a mentor, and he is sitting on your board, that's a good thing. [But] it doesn't guarantee selection. I can't tell you how many times I've heard "somebody's guy" came to the board and didn't get selected.

Even though you may be known by a number of the board members, performance still outweighs personal knowledge. Admiral R observed:

> Performance is key. You can have friends, you can have sponsors, and they will have some influence particularly if someone knows you and can speak personally about your attributes; that's a benefit. But, if your performance has not been of flag caliber, you won't get selected by the board.

Where all things are equal, people are more likely to select someone they know versus someone they do not. Admiral Q put it bluntly:

> Knowledge—that's human nature. To discredit that means you're stupid. "Hey, I know him. He's proven. This guy I don't know, he looks good, but if I have to make a choice, I'm picking my guy."

One way that some officers attempt to compensate for not having been in positions of high visibility is to obtain letters of recommendation from active and retired flag officers. The consensus was that, if an officer needed letters to recommend his selection, the message being sent to the board was that there was a problem in his record. An officer with a good record will be promoted based on the quality of his record, and not by the volume of recommendation letters. According to Admiral E:

> Letters in general ... don't add or subtract from the board. And [they are there] normally because the guy's in trouble. I mean, if you've got the record, and you've got the jobs, you don't need the letters. The record stands on its own. If, however, you were [rated] "3 of 4" in your major command, then maybe you need the letters to point out clearly that the only reason you were "3 of 4" was that this guy was CO of

---

[4]Members of the board cannot offer negative information about a candidate that is not included in his official record.

the carrier, and this guy was that, and you were new on the job, and it wasn't explained on the Fitness Report.

All of the interviewees expressed the difficulty of making the final selections. The interviewees agreed that any candidate within the final 100 selectees would probably make a good flag officer; the ones that were finally selected were those who had the right mix of reputation, background experience, and the requirements set in the precept. Admiral B summed it up well when he stated:

> That last bit, going from 100 to 25 is excruciating ... The reason for this is that all these guys are all fully qualified and should be flag officers for the good of the Navy. They've all done something that the Navy needs.

At this point, community reputation weighs heavily, as the qualifications among officers are often similar, if not identical.

Overall, selection boards were described as being fair. Although some officers who are not selected may believe that they were unfairly treated, the admirals in this study believed strongly that this was not the case. As Admiral N explained:

> You can't take personality out of it, but the board is a very, very good tool. Very few times have I ever seen it where it was a vindictive thing or anything like that. It was usually very professional. When you get to be an admiral, you want to take care of your Navy, and you want the best guys to be there. You've got to be fair.

Selection Board Considerations

In addition to discussing the overall selection board process, the admirals were asked to address consideration given to various background or career experiences of the flag nominees. Specifically, the interviews probed for whether commissioning source, graduate education, joint experience, FITREP scores, reputation, career timing, and other competencies were considered explicitly in the promotion decisions.

Commissioning source.   Although the literature and archival data suggest an Academy bias (cf. Bowman, 1991; Moore & Trout, 1978), the interviewees all denied any propensity on the part of selection boards to select USNA alumni. According to the archival data, 56% of flag officers in the sample from YGs 1972 through 1978 graduated from the USNA. Among the 18 submarine flag officers in the sample, only 4 were not USNA alumni. Commissioning sources for other communities can be seen in Table 2.

Table 3 shows the numbers of officers promoted to flag rank as contrasted to officers produced by each accession source for FY 1972 through 1975. Regardless of their own commissioning source, the interviewees noted without hesitation that

TABLE 2
Flag Officers by Commissioning Source

Community	Commissioning Source	n	%
NFO[a]	USNA	8	42
	ROTC	5	26
	OCS	5	26
Pilot[b]	USNA	18	56
	ROTC	8	32
	OCS	6	19
Sub[c]	USNA	14	78
	ROTC	2	11
	OCS	2	11
SWO[d]	USNA	15	48
	ROTC	9	29
	OCS	7	23

Note. $N = 99$. One flag officer (NFO) in the study was commissioned by the Air Force Academy and is not included in the table. NFO = naval flight officer; Sub = submarine; SWO = surface warfare officer; USNA = U.S. Naval Academy; ROTC = Reserve Officer Training Corps; OCS = Officer Candidate School.
[a]$n = 19$. [b]$n = 32$. [c]$n = 18$. [d]$n = 31$.

there was no special consideration given to commissioning source during the flag selection process. The tendency for USNA graduates to be amply represented among flag officers was attributed to implicit or moderating factors rather than explicit consideration. The particularly high percentage of USNA graduates among submariner flag officers was attributed to the rigorous engineering requirements and academic standards. Admiral C bluntly discounted an officer's commissioning source as a reason for selection:

> Given equal qualifications, it doesn't mean a damn where you graduated; the "ring-knocker" stuff is a bunch of crap. I have never seen that in selection boards.

Similarly, according to Admiral J, a non-Academy graduate:

> I never heard a derogatory comment about a commissioning source, and I never heard the Naval Academy, for example, as a reason, at all, to support our selection.

Graduate education.   In contrast to equivocal evidence from the literature and archival data regarding the importance of graduate education, as discussed earlier, interviewees were much more positive. Although graduate education is important, it may be outweighed by other performance variables in selection to flag rank. A surprisingly high number of flag officers in the sample (29%) did not have a graduate degree (Table 4). Yet, according to Admiral L:

TABLE 3
Flag Officers by Commissioning Source, Year Groups 1972–1975[a]

Year Group	Source	URL Flags	Officers Commissioned[b]	% of Commissioning Source	% of Year Group Total
1972	USNA	9	739	1.22	0.26
	OCS	6	1,692	0.35	0.18
	ROTC	3	991	0.30	0.09
	Total	18	3,422	0.53	
1973	USNA	11	725	1.52	0.38
	OCS	2	1,291	0.15	0.07
	ROTC	5	852	0.59	0.17
	Total	18	2,868	0.63	
1974	USNA	12	822	1.46	0.43
	OCS	5	915	0.55	0.18
	ROTC	5	1,057	0.47	0.18
	Total	22	2,794	0.79	
1975	USNA	14	700	2.00	0.48
	OCS	5	1,134	0.44	0.17
	ROTC	4	1,074	0.37	0.14
	Total	23	2,908	0.79	

Note. URL = unrestricted line; USNA = U.S. Naval Academy; OCS = Officer Candidate School; ROTC = Reserve Officer Training Corps; RL = restricted line.
[a]Year Groups 1976 to 1978 are not included because flag selections from these year groups were still possible at the time of data collection for this study. Flag selections for 1972 to 1975 are complete.
[b]Reflects the total number of URL and RL officers commissioned.

Graduate education is important along the way because one, it can put you into a subspecialty that is important to the Navy and two, it's a discriminator. Without it, it's easy for someone to say at some future board: "He doesn't have a master's degree." Because having one is the norm, not having one means it's unusual, and you don't want to ever have something unusual in a negative sense.

Admiral H saw graduate education as a definitive need in today's environment:

In this world, it is a very rare circumstance for an individual whose undergraduate experience will carry him all the way through. I think it's wrong to make it an on–off switch but it's very important for the needs of the Navy to have individuals who are … educated beyond the undergraduate level.

Staff/joint/operational experience. In addition to aptitude and education, experience is vital for attaining flag rank. All of the flag officers in the study had attained their requisite warfare milestones, including command and major com-

TABLE 4
Number of Graduate Degrees Held by Flag Officers in the Sample

	None		One		Two		Three		PhD	
	n	%	n	%	n	%	n	%	n	%
SWO	5	15	17	50	6	18	1	3	2	6
Sub	6	29	10	48	2	10	0	0	0	0
Pilot	9	26	19	54	2	6	1	3	1	3
NFO	9	47	7	37	2	11	1	5	0	0
Total	29	29	53	53	12	12	3	3	3	3

Note.   SWO = surface warfare officer; Sub = submarine; NFO = naval flight officer.

mand. The importance of command was noted by all of those interviewed. In discussing the attributes of command, Admiral F said:

> One of the things I looked for in promotions into the flag community: I was looking for somebody, quite frankly, that had been stress-tested. There are many paths to flag, and some of them are more stressful than others. Quite frankly, I think that for being a flag officer—not questioning the moral character or ethics that go along with tough decision making—the next best attribute or quality that one should look at is how they handled the tremendous weight of responsibility. Those who have been through these stress-laden positions and have weathered them well and excelled in that environment generally will do well as a flag officer.

However, doing well at sea does not guarantee selection to flag rank. Too much time at sea, in fact, can actually become a detriment to an officer's career. At the flag officer level, the ability to plan battle groups is in demand rather than ship driving. That is, strategic planning is sought rather than tactical operations.

Further, command at sea is not the only "proving" tour for an officer; the overall challenge of the job is considered. Interviewees also encouraged variety in a career background. As Admiral Q cautioned, there is a delicate balance between variety and depth; that is, one must avoid getting too much variety at the expense of knowledge depth:

> Variety is a huge positive factor. The more exposure you get, joint, operational, education, the more positive ... A lot of times [however], the guy who's interested in punching the ticket has a lot of variety, but has no depth. The real key is to find a guy who has a lot of variety in positions with depth.

The interviewees validated the visibility hypothesis or accumulating distinguishing career characteristics as important considerations for flag promotion. Executive assistant (EA) jobs were noted as a key means by which many officers gain both the experience and the visibility for future flag selection. Admiral C commented:

> The executive assistant has the advantage—or disadvantage—of being very visible and having a lot of interface with people more senior than he. There, clearly, you either have a chance to fall on your sword or be more widely known professionally. When I was selected for flag rank, there was no one on the flag board at the time I hadn't interfaced with in the course of my professional assignments. Is that an advantage? I think so. You're a known entity.

It is important to keep in mind that the EA tour itself does not lead to flag selection. Only proven, top performers are put in that role. These jobs are the ones into which the best officers are placed. The interviewees noted that the EA was simply a way to learn the top-level practices of the Navy.

Whereas the jobs officers have throughout their career can broaden their backgrounds and give them the requisite experiences for flag selection, it is how they perform in the job that really makes a difference in their chances for selection. Performance is documented by the Navy's FITREP process.

Fitness reports. FITREPs play a vital role in the selection process. There are three portions of a FITREP: a numerical trait average on a scale of 1 to 5, a section for comments from the rating officer, and a section for ranking an officer against peers. This latter section, by far, carries the most weight in the selection process. The section that holds secondary importance is the comments section. Finally, the trait averages are expected to be perfect for an officer competitive for flag selection because of grade inflation as well as the true stellar performance of the candidate. Any significant deviation from top marks as a senior officer would send a negative message to the board.

Two other important aspects of a FITREP are the person who wrote the FITREP and the presence (or lack) of a flag promotion recommendation. A glowing FITREP from an O10 far outweighs a similarly stellar FITREP written by an O4, simply because of the experience level and reputation of the writer. Flag promotion recommendations are a single line or two that recommend that the flag selection board promote the officer to flag. If these statements are not present in the FITREP of a senior officer before the flag selection board, it conveys an extremely negative message to the board.

Members of the flag board read hundreds of FITREPs during the course of a flag selection board. The wording becomes vital, as described by Admiral E:

> How do you catch the guy who's on his 100th record ... and every record has had eight fitness reports? How do you get him to sit up and say: "I'm going to look at this one" ... Most people read the first paragraph, and read the last paragraph. If they find

something they were really interested in, they might go back and read: "Little Johnny was Electrical Officer for six months." Fine, but what did you really think about Little Johnny? And you put that in the first paragraph, and the last paragraph. And that's where it says: "Recommended for Flag" or ... "If I had to go to war, this is the guy I'd want with me." Lines like that stick. They get their attention ... I can document what you've done ... What I really want to document is your potential. Where are you going? What's your future in the Navy? ... That's what the board is looking for.

One of the things that makes a FITREP stand out is a recommendation to promote the officer to flag rank. Admiral F also discussed the importance of the recommendation:

Without it, they wouldn't be considered. That's an important indication. It's more of a signal, it's a note to say: "Do look at this report more carefully because of that recommendation."

Admiral C also noted the importance of rankings on the FITREPs, and the drawback of not having a large group to be rated against:

I put a lot more stock in the comparative markings than I did in the actual markings. I think most people do. Somebody who stands out as one of the top 3 people in a group of 20 is more important in assessing his ability than the fact that he's got perfect marks and he's a 1 of 1.

Admiral E agreed:

If a guy is always 1 of 1, and never gets competed with, that's not good either. You can be the best in the world, but if you never compete with the other talent [it has a detrimental effect].

Several interviewees discussed how the rankings played a large part in the determination of which records would be removed from further consideration on the flag board. However, in addition to the ratings, the author of the FITREP is salient. According to Admiral N:

One of the big things that carries a lot of weight ... is who wrote the fitness report. I know it sounds ... like nepotism, but very frankly, very few of us got to make admiral because we were so much better than the guy who didn't ... If you have a guy who's coming up and all of a sudden the guy who wrote his fitness reports was the guy who was CNO, was CINCPACFLT,[5] and this and that and all of them said the same thing over a period of years, that's kind of important.

---

[5]Commander in Chief, Pacific Fleet, now Commander, Pacific Fleet (COMPACFLT), an O10 position.

Just as the reputation of the FITREP signer is important, the reputation of the officer coming before the selection board is just as important.

Reputation.   An officer's reputation may be one of the most important attributes weighed in the flag selection process. Some interviewees considered this the most important variable in selection, as it had a direct positive or negative effect on the career of an officer to that point. Although an officer's reputation starts as a junior officer, the point at which it becomes well known is at the executive officer (XO) and commanding officer (CO) levels. Admiral H detailed how the importance of reputation grows throughout the career of an officer:

> As the pyramid gets more narrow, there is an additional factor, service reputation, which is beyond what's just written on the paper, beyond the marks and beyond the comments ... as the community, as the individuals about whom you're talking gets smaller ... your reputation among your subordinates your peers and your superiors is going to become more and more well known, and it counts as a factor in the selection process.

Career timing.   Another vital factor in the selection of an officer to flag rank is career timing. Officers are expected to achieve certain milestones in their career progression within a specific time frame. Sometimes, if an officer is too early, or conversely, too late, in his career timing, it may make him ineligible for certain jobs requisite for continued promotion. Another effect that career timing can have is in the competencies of an officer. Some officers have skills that were in demand earlier in their careers, but as they moved into the more senior ranks, their skills became obsolete, such as skills in flying a decommissioned aircraft type, or specialization in a certain program that was later canceled.

Early promotions are not always beneficial in flag promotion. For a select few officers, early promotions in the junior ranks can speed them on a path to attaining flag rank at a younger age, thus allowing for more years of service as a flag officer before retirement becomes necessary. However, for many officers, early promotion thrusts them into positions of responsibility for which they were not yet fully prepared (or miss entirely), causing them to perform poorly, and thus hindering their chances at future promotion. The majority felt that the potential for early promotions to harm a career was greater than their potential to help it. Admiral K noted:

> Early promotions can be a tremendous thing for the person who got to the opportunity to see stuff. But, for the person it short-sheets of experience where they're now going to compete with guys that have had a joint tour, or have worked on that staff and know how the boss is going to be thinking, versus this brilliant kid ... I guess it can go either way. I've seen it go wonderfully well for the Navy with folks like Admiral [name deleted] who didn't need as much time as me to assimilate the lessons

learned at that particular rank or in that particular job ... But there are just as many who get thrown into that next job and all of a sudden are not as effective ... because they missed out on a stepping stone or perhaps they stopped being a lifelong learner ... I've seen it go both ways.

Competencies and personality. Competencies mentioned as valuable by the interviewees included people and political skills. These less obvious characteristics include such things as not continually looking for promotions, being able to interface well with both subordinates and superiors and others, and the ability to speak well and articulate their thoughts and positions, among many others.

Admiral L discussed the importance of being able to think and perform at a higher level. He also mentioned the importance of learning how to operate within a bureaucracy:

> To anticipate your boss's needs, to anticipate how he should interact or think through how the most useful way to present information to him so that he can understand the issue and so that he can articulate the issue or defend the position or react to somebody ... The other thing is understanding the bureaucracy. You have to serve in it to understand it ... You have to have a sense of politics and how people react in a bureaucracy; where power lies, what you can do, and what you can't do—how to get things done.

Admiral C discussed personality factors valuable for flag rank:

> We certainly prefer the outgoing personality to one who's living in a shell, we certainly prefer the person who is self-confident, with a basis for it, to one who is constantly looking over his shoulder, or wondering if this is the "right" thing to do. We certainly aren't interested in the one who worries everyday in whether or not he's promotable, who instead is paying attention to what his job requires. You want the person who'll do what's right, regardless of the consequences.

Admiral N discussed the factors he looked for at flag levels:

> I looked very hard at how he handled his people. There are guys out there who get the job done but there are a lot of body bags along the way—just "peoplekillers." Those are not the kind of guys who I would want to be flag ... There are some guys out there who look at the job they are in as just a stepping stone to the next job. I think that's a mistake. I think anybody can come from behind and make admiral, as long as you keep doing every job right as you go along. You can know right away by looking them in the eye if they are looking for the next job. The next part may sound silly to some people: I looked for guys with a lot of stamina. And I don't just mean physical stamina, but mental stamina. They could pursue things night and day and just didn't give up. Not everybody has that.

TABLE 5
Summary of Career Characteristics
and Their Impact on Flag Selection

Characteristic		Impact
1	Commissioning source	Low
2	Graduate education	Medium
3	Staff/joint/operational experience	High
3a	Command	Mandatory
3b	Joint experience	Mandatory
3c	Washington experience	High
3d	Executive assistant	High
4	Fitness reports	High
4a	Trait averages	Medium
4b	Comments	High
4c	Rankings	High
5	Reputation	High
6	Career timing	Low
7	Competencies and personality	Medium

Admiral I identified intellectual competency as a consideration for flag selection:

> That's another thing that runs though the thread of the flag board, kind of in the background, intellectually, is the guy intellectually capable of retaining large amounts of information and making sense out of them.

Summary.   Table 5 presents a summary of the interviewees' assessment of the relevance of various characteristics for flag officer selection.

DISCUSSION

A content analysis of 18 interviews with retired flag officers who had experience with flag officer selection boards together with a review of archival data revealed that reputation, FITREPs, and critical experience are key to such promotion decisions.

An officer's service reputation plays a critical role in selection to flag rank. An officer with a stellar record but a poor reputation has little chance of selection. An officer with an excellent reputation will be given close scrutiny, even if his record is not the best of the candidate pool. An officer's service reputation is a function of competencies and personality, and becomes known over the years by gaining staff, joint, and operational experience. Officers who demonstrate stellar performance in critical or complex operational assignments and who are well known in a positive manner among their peers and subordinates are evaluated favorably. Personal knowledge of and expression of high regard for flag candidates can make a positive contribution in the selection process.

Documented performance via FITREPs weighs heavily in an officer's selection to flag. In addition to stellar trait averages, a FITREP must have a specific recommendation for flag promotion. Although it is technically possible for an officer to be selected without this recommendation, such a record will fall under close scrutiny to ensure that the reporting officers who omitted it are not sending a covert message to the members of the board regarding that officer's selection potential. The officer's standing in peer rankings is also important. Competitive FITREPs are those with a majority of "1 of" and "2 of" rankings, particularly in the senior ranks. Assignments and experience certainly have a tremendous impact on the selection of an officer to flag rank. Two milestones are mandated: command at sea (specifically major command) and joint qualifications. Without these, an officer will not be considered.

Although graduate education is an important aspect of the career development of an officer, holding a graduate degree currently does not seem to have a critical impact on selection to flag rank. Similarly, commissioning source is reported not to have a direct effect on achieving flag rank.

Findings that flag officer promotion decisions are based on an earned reputation, documented performance, and critical experience in demanding assignments should come as no surprise. Retired admirals emphatically counter cynical anecdotes that the process is unfair, arbitrary, and capricious. It is not just who you know and where you went to school but what you know and what you did that counts. The relatively high representation of USNA graduates among flag officers is explained plausibly as an indirect effect of intellectual prowess and academic achievement as well as motivation. That is, USNA graduates are competitive because they have succeeded in meeting the Academy's stringent admission standards and graduation requirements. A known reputation and personal knowledge by a board member should be expected among flag candidates. According to the interviewees, the information conveyed from personal knowledge is job related and behaviorally anchored.

This qualitative study provides a rare glimpse into flag officer selection. The findings highlight the multiple, relevant dimensions weighed for flag candidates, counter some preconceived notions (e.g., commissioning source is not an explicit criterion for promotion), and unravel a few confounds. Although appropriate for exploratory purposes or to gain initial insights, the methodology and results from this study require elaboration. Although used only as a backdrop for this study, an analysis of records from those selected and not selected for flag is warranted. An evaluation and comparison of the presence and strength of key indicators as identified in this study should be conducted. Further elucidation of specific competencies and personality traits deemed important for flag officers is also required. A better understanding of the salient characteristics and critical dimensions of such subjective factors as FITREP statements and their authors would further demystify the flag selection process. With further study, more structure could be introduced into the flag officer screening and selection process. Such standardization of rating dimensions and scales would further ensure procedural justice and offer more concrete career guidance to prospective flag officers.

REFERENCES

Bowman, W. R. (1991). *Are service academies worth the cost? Recent findings for Navy warfare officers.* Annapolis, MD: U.S. Naval Academy.

Bowman, W. R., & Mehay. S. L. (1999). Graduate education and employee performance: Evidence from military personnel. *Economics of Education Review, 18,* 453–463.

Brancato, K., Harrell, M. C., Schirmer, P., & Thie, H. J. (2004). *Aligning the stars: Improvements to general and flag officer management.* Santa Monica, CA: Rand.

Buterbaugh, T. A. (1995). *A multivariate analysis of the effects of academic performance and graduate education on the promotion of senior U.S. Navy officers.* Unpublished master's thesis, Naval Postgraduate School, Monterey, CA.

Byham, W. C., Paese, M. J., & Smith, A. B. (2002). *Grow your own leaders.* Upper Saddle River, NJ: Prentice-Hall.

Cymrot, D. J. (1986). *Graduate education and the promotion of officers* (CNA Research Memorandum). Alexandria, VA: Center for Naval Analysis.

Eitelberg, M. J., Laurence, J. H., & Brown, D. C. (1992). Becoming brass: Issues in the testing, recruiting, and selection of American military officers. In B. R. Gifford & L. C. Wing (Eds.), *Test policy in defense: Lessons from the military for education, training, and employment* (pp. 79–219). Norwell, MA: Kluwer Academic.

Janowitz. M. (1971). *The professional soldier.* New York: Macmillan.

Kotter, J. P. (1982). *The general managers.* New York: The Free Press.

Moore, D. W., & Trout, B. T. (1978). Military advancement: The visibility theory of promotion. *American Political Science Review, 72,* 452–468.

Reynolds, C. G. (2002). *Famous American admirals.* Annapolis, MD: U.S. Naval Institute.

Savage, D. M. (1992). *Joint duty prerequisite for promotion to general/flag officer* (USAWC Military Studies Program paper). Carlisle Barracks, PA: U.S. Army War College.

Walsh, D. J. (1997). *Joint professional military education and its effects on the unrestricted line naval officer career.* Unpublished master's thesis, Naval Postgraduate School, Monterey, CA.

Woelper, E. P. (1998). *The impacts of academic background on submariner performance, retention and promotion.* Unpublished master's thesis, Naval Postgraduate School, Monterey, CA.

MILITARY PSYCHOLOGY, 2006, *18*(Suppl.), S103–S109

Implementation of Developmental Leadership in the Swedish Armed Forces

Gerry Larsson

Department of Leadership and Management
Swedish National Defence College
Karlstad, Sweden

The impact of behavioral research on military systems design is often limited. Typically, military, technical, economic, and political systems designers are more influential. The implementation of a new leadership model—developmental leadership—in the Swedish Armed Forces may constitute an exception. The aim of this article is to describe and evaluate the implementation process and its effects. The new leadership model is now well on the way to full-scale implementation. The conclusion is that an interplay between structural aspects (limited organization size and the formal authority of the supreme commander) and behavioral and attitudinal aspects (internal and external change agents) contributed to this outcome.

Successful implementation of organizational change programs typically involves multimodal efforts including structural, behavioral, and attitudinal components. Structural changes alone often lack a necessary motivational component. Behavioral and attitudinal changes alone often depend on enthusiastic change agents and tend to fade when they leave the scene (Huse & Cummings, 1975).

Possibly due to an underrating of the importance of structural components, the impact of behavioral research on military systems design and change is frequently perceived as limited by those of us who are involved in it. Typically, we enter the field one step behind the military, technical, economic, and political systems designers. However, in one area of systems design—military leader selection and development—the last years represent an exception to this rule. Behavioral researchers at the Swedish National Defence College (SNDC) developed a new system, labeled developmental leadership (see Larsson et al., 2003, for details), and ac-

Correspondence should be addressed to Gerry Larsson, Department of Leadership and Management, Swedish National Defence College, Karolinen, SE-651 80 Karlstad, Sweden. E-mail: gerry .larsson@fhs.se

tively participated in its implementation in the Swedish Armed Forces (SAF). The aim of this chapter is to describe and evaluate the implementation process and its effects.

DESCRIPTION OF THE IMPLEMENTATION PROCESS

Initial Steps

In 1997, three colleagues (see Acknowledgments) and I formed the Military Leadership Group (MLG). In later years, three more colleagues joined the group. We represented different academic backgrounds (pedagogics, psychology, and sociology) and different professions (behavioral scientist, military officer, psychiatrist, psychologist, and sociologist). A strong interest in leadership tied us together. We pooled different kinds of funding from the SAF (and later also the Swedish Rescue Services) to finance our efforts.

Later in 1997, we entered a transformational leadership course as participants, run by Professors Bernard Bass and Bruce Avolio. They kindly offered us plenty of advice. After this, in 1998, a group of Swedish researchers and military officers went on a study trip to Israel. The Israeli Defense Force had begun implementing a slightly modified version of transformational leadership. Once more, we were generously offered help on how to conduct the training, and colleagues from Israel, headed by Dr. Reuven Gal, later came to Sweden a number of times to give additional advice.

In 1999, we arranged an international conference on transformational leadership in military contexts. The participants, including Professors Bass and Avolio and our Israeli colleagues, came from about 10 countries.

The initial steps also included a translation into Swedish of the Multifactor Leadership Questionnaire (MLQ revised form 5x; Avolio & Bass, 1998). Computer programming of individual feedback reports and checking of formal contracts were other early ingredients.

Development of a 360°-Based Course

A leadership development course was created. The original course content drew heavily on the outline of transformational leadership courses. Before a course, each participant conducts a self-rating (a Swedish translation of the MLQ was initially used). In the typical case, he or she is also rated by one superior, two individuals at the same organizational level, and three subordinates. During a 2-day course, the participants learn the model, receive feedback from the questionnaire responses, and create a personal development plan. A 1-day booster session follows 2 to 3 months later.

Two Strategic Pilot Courses

The implementation process continued with two pilot courses in 1999. The first consisted of about 15 leadership teachers from the Swedish military academies. The second consisted of about 15 Swedish colonels. Both groups were carefully selected. We offered the course to leadership teachers and colonels who had a reputation for being progressive and influential. Both courses were favorably received by the participants.

Parallel Activities

Development of a Swedish questionnaire. A problem we frequently encountered during the initial leadership courses was that the MLQ items were perceived as "too American." This is not a criticism, but merely a realization that the two cultures differ. Thus, after several modifications of the original translation, in 2001 we finally rewrote all the items. The aim was to design items that covered the content of the factors and facets of the model as it gradually developed. The instrument was labeled the Developmental Leadership Questionnaire (DLQ), and it has proved to have satisfactory psychometric properties (Larsson, in press; Larsson et al., 2003).

Another strong motive for creating a Swedish instrument was that the SAF, for self-evident reasons, were reluctant to have the questionnaires of Swedish officers being processed by a private company in the United States.

Training of trainers. It soon became apparent that the capacity of the MLG was inadequate from an implementation point of view. Therefore, a course for the training of trainers was developed in 2001 and gradually refined.

Courses in other contexts. Through informal initiatives, courses were also being held in contexts such as the Swedish Rescue Services, the Swedish police, the Swedish Governmental Office, and the Norwegian Armed Forces.

A new system for leader evaluation. In 2000, the SAF decided to develop a new system for the annual evaluation of military officers. The task was given to research colleagues at the SNDC. In collaboration, it was decided to use the developmental leadership model for this purpose. This means that identical criteria of goodness and badness are used in the evaluation and the development contexts. It also means that all officers are confronted with the concepts of the model on an annual basis.

A new book on military leadership. In 1999 I was appointed as editor of a new book on leadership for the SAF. This book (Larsson & Kallenberg, 2003) is based on the developmental leadership model.

The breakthrough.   After a series of presentations of the manuscript of the new leadership book to military officers at successively higher hierarchical levels at the SAF Headquarters, a meeting was held with the Swedish Supreme Commander early in 2003. The outcome was favorable, as he said "yes" to the book as well as to the developmental leadership concept. It was decided that this concept should prevail from April 1, 2003. We were given the task of developing an implementation strategy.

Components of the Implementation Strategy

An implementation strategy was formulated by the researchers in the MLG, assisted by military officers from a group within the SAF Headquarters called the Leadership and Pedagogic Unit. This strategy is summarized in the following sections.

Basic strategy—Top-down approach and training of trainers.   An ideal implementation strategy was formulated. It was intended to be used at all military academies, staffs, and regiments. It consisted of the following four steps: (a) a developmental leadership course for the top management group; (b) the top management selects two to four suitable trainers from the organization, each of whom should have leadership teaching skills and high credibility; (c) training of the selected trainers; and (d) leadership courses conducted by these trainers with the rest of the organization.

Legal aspects.   Law experts from the SAF assisted in the formulation of written contracts between the SAF and the SNDC, as well as between the individual trainers and the SNDC.

Personal briefings.   Informal personal briefings were held with the brigadier at the SAF Headquarters who was responsible for the military school system. They were followed up with lectures when he had national meetings with officers from the military academies, staffs, and regiments.

Popular writings.   Popular articles presenting developmental leadership were written by the MLG and published in Swedish military journals. A link to a popular description of the model was also added to the SNDC Internet home page.

Continued research.   Two different lines of continued research have been followed. One is focused on improvement of the DLQ (Larsson, in press). The other is oriented toward leadership in indirect form at higher hierarchical levels (Larsson, Sjöberg, Vrbanjac, & Björkman, 2005).

Armed Forces Downsizing: A Confounder

We now had the formal decision and an implementation plan, but the actual implementation was still proceeding slowly. A major reason for this was probably a heavy downsizing of the SAF. Thousands of military officers left for civilian jobs. Among them were a number of those we had trained as trainers. In 2005 the situation improved somewhat, and there are now more than 150 licensed trainers.

Sexual Harassment: An Unexpected Boost

During the last 6 months, military officers in the SAF have been involved in a number of sexual harassment scandals. In April 2005, the supreme commander initiated a series of actions to handle the problem. One of these actions was a decision to have licenced developmental leadership trainers at all military regiments, staffs, and schools by July 1, 2006. We expect this decision to advance the implementation process further.

EVALUATION OF THE IMPLEMENTATION PROCESS AND ITS EFFECTS

Current Status

In summary, colleagues at the SNDC are now actively running a system for the training of trainers, they have improved the pedagogical concept, and they are finalizing the work on a Web-based version of the DLQ. The leadership book mentioned previously is being used at all military academies in Sweden. The implementation of the new system for leader evaluation (see preceding) continues as well. Assuming that the implementation process will go on as planned, it would mean that a behavioral research effort has had a noticeable impact on an entire military organization. The final section of this article is devoted to some reflections on this.

Structural Aspects

Organization size.   These days, Sweden has a comparatively small military organization with about 10,000 military officers. Compared to countries with bigger organizations, it seems reasonable to assume that the limited size offers more favorable conditions for organization transformation.

Formal authority.   In a hierarchical system such as a military organization, decisions made by the highest executive leader must be regarded as a strong formal source of influence. In the case of developmental leadership, we received formal support twice from this level (see earlier).

Behavioral and Attitudinal Aspects

Internal change agents. The conscious selection of progressive leaders and leadership teachers has most likely contributed to the implementation process. Through their enthusiasm and influence, the concept has been spread with a positive touch. Currently, I venture to guess that the vast majority of military and civilian personnel in the SAF know about developmental leadership.

External change agents. The close collaboration between researchers at the SNDC and internal change agents in the SAF may also have had an impact on the implementation. Regular formal and informal contacts with the licensed trainers are part of this collaboration. The new book on leadership and the new system for annual evaluation are additional contributions from the external change agents.

CONCLUSIONS

The developmental leadership model is well on the way to full-scale implementation in the SAF. The conclusion is that an interplay between structural aspects (limited organization size and the formal authority of the Swedish Supreme Commander) and behavioral and attitudinal aspects (internal and external change agents) contributed to this outcome. The available evaluation data (subjective ratings and lived experiences) suggest that much use of developmental leadership behaviors has favorable performance effects.

ACKNOWLEDGMENTS

I thank my colleagues Lars Andersson, Erna Danielsson, Ann Johansson, Eva Johansson, Per-Olof Michel, and Ingemar Robertson. Together we created the developmental leadership model, the DLQ, and all took an active part in the implementation process.

REFERENCES

Avolio, B. J., & Bass, B. M. (1998). *The full range of leadership development: Basic and advanced manuals.* Binghamton, NY: Bass, Avolio & Associates.

Huse, W. F., & Cummings, T. G. (1975). *Organization development and change.* New York: West.

Larsson, G. (in press). The Developmental Leadership Questionnaire (DLQ): Some psychometric properties. *Scandinavian Journal of Psychology.*

Larsson, G., Carlstedt, L., Andersson, J., Andersson, L., Danielsson, E., Johansson, A., et al. (2003). A comprehensive system for leader evaluation and development. *Leadership & Organization Development Journal, 24,* 16–25.

Larsson, G., & Kallenberg, K. (Eds.). (2003). *Direkt ledarskap* [Direct leadership]. Stockholm, Sweden: Försvarsmakten.

Larsson, G., Sjöberg, M., Vrbanjac, A., & Björkman, T. (2005). Indirect leadership: A qualitative study on how to do it. *Leadership & Organization Development Journal, 26,* 215–227.

MILITARY PSYCHOLOGY, 2006, *18*(Suppl.), S111–S129
Copyright © 2006, Lawrence Erlbaum Associates, Inc.

OPERATIONS

Performance-Shaping Factors Associated With Navigation Accidents in the Royal Norwegian Navy

Kristian S. Gould
Section for Occupational Medicine
Faculty of Medicine
University of Bergen, Norway

Bjarte Knappen Røed
The Royal Norwegian Navy Navigation Centre
The Royal Norwegian Naval Academy
Bergen, Norway

Vilhelm F. Koefoed
Commander Naval Medicine
The Royal Norwegian Navy
Bergen, Norway

Robert S. Bridger
Human Factors Division
Institute of Naval Medicine
Alverstoke, United Kingdom

Bente E. Moen
Section for Occupational Medicine
Faculty of Medicine
University of Bergen, Norway

Correspondence should be addressed to Kristian S. Gould, University of Bergen, Faculty of Medicine, Section for Occupational Medicine, Kalfarveien 31, 5018 Bergen. Norway. E-mail: kristian .gould@isf.uib.no

This study examined the presence of performance-shaping factors (PSFs) in investigation reports following 35 navigation accidents in the Royal Norwegian Navy between 1990 and 2005. This was done to provide an overview of the situational factors present at the time of the accidents, which were related to the human, task, system, and environment. PSFs are defined as any factors that influence the likelihood of an error occurring. Factors related to task requirements and individual cognitive characteristics were most common, followed by operational characteristics of the system. Eight PSF clusters were found, indicating a pattern in accident circumstances. Possible measures for improving safety and performance include training, changes in task organization, and improved bridge systems.

Accidents at sea pose a considerable threat to the safety of people and the environment, and can be very costly. Human-related causes account for a large portion of maritime accidents; it has been estimated that human error costs the maritime industry $541 million a year (The Nautical Institute, 2003). Yet few systematic studies of human factors in naval ship accidents have been carried out. Research on aviation, road traffic, and rail accidents is comparatively extensive, allowing a better understanding of the issues related to their causes (Fuller & Santos, 2002; Sarter & Amalberti, 2000; Wilson et al., 2001). Insurance statistics from merchant shipping have shown that a large proportion of claims following navigation accidents involve human-related malfunction; the U.K. P&I Club insurance group has attributed 62% of its total major claims over a 15-year period to human error (The Nautical Institute, 2003).

Cockroft (1984) reported that about 90% of all marine accidents happen in confined waters such as channels and inshore traffic zones. The inshore coast of Norway is arguably one of the most challenging navigation areas in the world, characterized by extreme weather; long periods of darkness; and thousands of islets, shallows, and narrow straits (Kjerstad, 2002). The complexity of navigation in such waters places a high demand on operators, especially with regard to factors such as multiple task performance and handling situations with a great level of uncertainty (Hockey, Healey, Crawshaw, Wastell, & Sauer, 2003).

Performance-shaping factors (PSFs) are factors "which influence the likelihood of an error occurring" (Kirwan, 1998, p. 157). PSFs are rooted in the premise that human behavior is influenced by the conditions at any time, and that these conditions can be identified as individual factors. In the context of human reliability, it is assumed that these factors influence performance, but do not necessarily determine it (Hollnagel, 1998). A PSF can therefore be considered to be either a cause or a contributor to unsafe actions in an accident review (Kim & Jung, 2003). In this article, no distinction has been made between PSFs that were likely to have caused the mishap, contributed to it, or had no influence on the course of events. It is impossible to separate causal factors from contributing factors, as both are necessary for a mishap to occur (Dekker, 2002).

Post hoc studies of PSFs in accidents have previously been carried out in aviation, the nuclear industry, and merchant shipping, for example (Sasou & Reason, 1999; Yacavone, 1993). Unfortunately, these studies have lacked information regarding the quality of the reports used as data, how the analyses were carried out, and which sources of bias may have influenced their results. Although all report-based accident reviews have a number of inherent weaknesses (Johnson, 2000), we have attempted to strengthen the validity of the results by using a consensus-based procedure, and clarifying the methodological limitations of our analysis.

The concept of the PSF has long existed as part of the human reliability assessment (HRA) methodology, but it is—broadly speaking—quite similar to the concepts of performance-influencing factors (PIFs), influencing factors (IFs), performance affecting factors (PAFs), error-producing conditions (EPCs), common performance conditions (CPCs), and so forth (Kim & Jung, 2003). These concepts originate from human reliability taxonomies, and have a common denominator in that they (a) describe causes or contributors to unsafe human actions in event analyses, and (b) provide a basis for evaluating human factors in safety assessments.

PSF data are particularly important at the present time, in light of increased performance capabilities of naval ships and the increased tactical focus on littoral (inshore) naval operations (Farris & Welch, 1998; Mulcahy, 2005). The U.S. Navy has already launched its HSV-X1 Joint Venture high-speed craft, which was used in Operation Iraqi Freedom (Holton, 2003). Other craft include the Royal Norwegian Navy (RNoN) Skjold-class fast patrol boats, the Swedish Navy's Visby-class, and the U.S. Navy's planned Littoral Combat Ship (Calvano et al., 2001). These vessels have a number of common features; most important, they have maximum speeds in excess of 35 kt, are operated by small crews, utilize electronic navigation systems, and are designed for littoral operations. The RNoN has vast experience with littoral operations and high-speed navigation, both being two cornerstones of its defensive capabilities. Unfortunately, the RNoN also has considerable experience with groundings, collisions, and other navigation accidents—resulting in substantial material costs, and occasionally, personal injury. Since 1989, the estimated incidence of major navigation mishaps in the RNoN has been around six vessels per year (Norwegian Ministry of Defence, 2005).

Prior human factors research on navigation accidents has largely been directed toward large merchant ships (e.g., Brigham, 1972; Wagenaar & Groeneweg, 1987). Recent studies by Kjerstad (2004) have focused on human factors in small high-speed vessels, which are functionally quite different from conventional merchant ships. Using a full-scale high-speed craft (HSC) simulator with a realistic coastal scenario, it was found that interface design strongly influenced navigators' performance when sailing a standard route under varying weather conditions. Student navigators also tended to underestimate safe speeds in many areas, and consequently, increased speed was shown to negatively influence the risk of grounding (Kjerstad, 2004).

We suggest that the navigation tasks usually performed in the RNoN and by crews of other littoral naval vessels are fundamentally different from those in both merchant shipping and civilian passenger HSCs, for the following reasons:

1. Naval vessels have unique tasks and operational demands that are different, and in many cases more intense, than on civilian ships.
2. RNoN vessels operate to a greater extent in shallow, poorly marked, or otherwise complicated waters at high speeds.
3. Many vessels do not operate with multiple shift systems, occasionally leading to extended periods of crew sleep deprivation.
4. RNoN crew members are generally younger and have a different educational background and level of experience compared to merchant mariners.
5. Bridge crews operate with different crew sizes and use different navigation principles than most merchant ships.

Research on navigation accidents is important for improving safety and performance not only in the RNoN, but also other naval fleets performing similar tasks.

Our primary aim for this study was to examine the presence of PSFs in navigation accidents in the RNoN during the period from 1990 to 2005. PSFs were not quantified (as in HRA), only identified. We wanted to develop an understanding of the PSFs associated with each accident to describe the situational context in which naval navigation accidents have occurred. Our secondary aim was to examine possible patterns in PSFs, by means of cluster analysis. The purpose for doing this was to see if navigation accidents could be classified into relatively unique categories, according to PSF clusters.

METHOD

Data

Our study set out to assess the PSFs found in navigation accidents in the RNoN between 1990 and 2005. Archival data were available only for this period. The archival data for the study consisted of all accident investigation reports produced by naval investigation committees and incident reports filed by the commanding officer (CO) on a ship following a navigation accident. The type of report produced following an incident is determined by internal RNoN regulations.

Accident investigations are generally instigated when personal injury has occurred, or material damages above 250,000 Norwegian krone have been incurred. The investigation committees usually consist of four to seven members, and are assembled by the Commander Naval Forces, Norway. The committee members are selected according to the individual circumstances for each incident, such as which type of ship was involved, if technical malfunctions were involved, or if any personal injuries occurred. At least one workers' representative is included (from the privates' or officers' unions), and a physician must be included in the case of injury. The commission members are not required to have any formal training in accident investigations. Their primary obligations are to determine (a) the events leading to the cause of the accident, (b) the cost of material damages resulting from the accident, and (c) how similar accidents might be prevented in the future. The information used to produce the final report is primarily obtained from witness interviews, track logs, and incident reports from the crew of the ship.

Incident reports are less extensive than accident investigation reports, and are based on self-reported information. The CO of a ship is required to file a report following a grounding, collision, or other mishap that does not satisfy the criteria for initiating a formal investigation. The report is based on general guidelines, and includes factual information about environmental conditions, the activities being undertaken, and the events leading up to the accident. To reduce selection bias from only including accident investigation reports, both types of reports were analyzed. The CO reports differ from the accident investigation reports in that they contain less detailed information, do not identify specific causes, and generally do not elaborate on issues beyond the sequence of actions leading to the accident.

We utilized an exploratory approach when selecting the PSFs to analyze in the accident reports. Most existing PSF taxonomies are closely tied to specific domains, such as nuclear power plants (THERP; Swain & Guttman, 1983) or chemical process plants (PHECA; Whalley, 1988). Thus, many taxonomies include PSFs that are either highly situation-specific (e.g., g-force effects and phase of plant operation), or do not adequately cover the range of PSFs that fit the characteristics of navigation. We therefore decided to follow the approach taken by Kim and Jung (2003), who constructed a situation-specific taxonomy (for nuclear emergency tasks) based on a full set of PSFs compiled from 18 existing PSF and HRA taxonomies. We adapted this approach by creating an equivalent PSF taxonomy for navigation tasks. We did this by extracting 109 PSFs from the original full set of 220 PSFs, which were collected from all taxonomies. Readers are referred to Kim and Jung for a comprehensive overview of the PSF and HRA taxonomies and the full PSF list.

We carried out the process of selecting the PSFs for our final taxonomy in cooperation with experienced RNoN accident investigators. The PSFs were selected according to the following criteria:

1. Relevance to the navigation tasks performed.
2. Concordance with available data in the accident reports.
3. Minimal overlap with other PSFs.

The final list of PSFs that we sought to identify in the accident reports in this study is shown in Table 1. The PSFs are presented according to the category structure

TABLE 1
List of Performance-Shaping Factors Analyzed in a Study of Navigation Accidents
in the Royal Norwegian Navy

Main Group	Subgroup	Detailed Items
1. Human	1.1 Cognitive Characteristics	1.1.1 Cognitive States Attention Skill level Knowledge Training Experience 1.1.2 Temporal Cognitive States Memory of recent actions Operator diagnosis Perceived importance Perceived consequences Operator expectations
	1.2 Physical and Psychological Characteristics	1.2.1 Physical States Fatigue 1.2.2 Psychological States Task burden
2. Task	2.1 Procedures	2.1.1 Procedure Quality Number of steps Required time for completion Clarity of instruction and terminology Level of standardization in use of terminology Number of simultaneous tasks Adequacy of caution/warning 2.1.2 Task Type Type of man–machine interface Required level of cognition Dynamic vs. step-by-step activities 2.1.3 Task Attributes/Requirements Amount of required information Information load Task difficulty Task novelty Frequency and familiarity of task Number of simultaneous goals/tasks Concurrent activities and interruptions Interruption from other personnel Discrepancy between training and reality Necessity of auxiliary tools Multiple sensory requirements Perceptual requirements Task criticality Physical requirements Degree of manual operations

(continued)

TABLE 1 (Continued)

Main Group	Subgroup	Detailed Items
		Motor requirements
		Muscular power
		Speed
		Dexterity
		Precision
		Calculational requirement
		Anticipatory requirement
		Requirement on and type of feedback
		Degree of reference to other materials than procedures
		Communication requirement
		Team cooperation requirement
3. System	3.1 Man–Machine Interface	3.1.1 Indicator/Controllers
		Availability
		Reliability
		Discrimination/distinguishability of signals
		Attributes
		Orientation
		Labeling
		Location
		Stuck instrument
		Conflicting signals/cues
		3.1.2 Panel/Screen Layout
		Reachability
		Visibility
		Coding/labeling
		Compatibility
		State of arrangement
		Complicatedness of panel(s)
		3.1.3 Support Systems
		Availability/adequacy
		Usability of required function
	3.2 System States	3.2.1 System States
		Inherent system complexity
		Organization of components
		Number of coupled components
		Reliability
		Redundancy
		Level of automation
		Stuck/failed components
	3.3 Phenomenological Characteristics	3.3.1 Operational Characteristics
		Suddenness of onset
		Overlap with previous tasks
		Time available for operator performance
		Time pressure (time required vs. time available)

(continue

TABLE 1 (Continued)

Main Group	Subgroup	Detailed Items
4. Environment	4.1 Physical Working Conditions	4.1.1 Physical Constraints Temperature/humidity/pressure Illumination Interferences in commmunication Noise Vibration Narrow work space or obstacles Accessibility of components 4.1.2 Timing Aspects Time of day Time on duty Circadian rhythm effects
	4.2 Team and Organization Factors	4.2.1 Team-Related Factors Clearness in job description or role definition Clearness in responsibilities/communication line Adequacy of distributed workload Intra/interteam cooperation Team cohesiveneness/collaboration Ability/leadership/authority of team leader Commitment to leadership 4.2.2 Team Communication-Related Factors Standardization in instruction/information delivery Media of instruction/information delivery Established protocol/form of instruction/information delivery Protocol between sender and receiver 4.2.3 Management and Policy Work (task) organization Shift organization Shift rotation Level of supervision Maintenance Quality assurance Safety measures Rewards and punishments Work methods 4.2.4 Safety Culture Routine violations Use of alcohol/drugs

Note.   Based on Kim and Jung (2003).

used by Kim and Jung (2003). Some PSFs excluded from our taxonomy could have been applicable if relevant data were available.

In addition to the PSFs, factual data regarding weather conditions, visibility, time of day, season, type of vessel, personal injury, technical malfunction, and activity were gathered from the reports.

Procedure

Accident reports were gathered from various archives of the RNoN and the Norwegian Ministry of Defence. There is currently no centralized database or archive for RNoN accident reports. Nonnavigational accidents (e.g., fires onboard and gunshot injuries) were excluded, as were incidents involving small boats (e.g., rigid inflatable boats) belonging to other military branches. The remaining 35 reports consisted of 24 accident investigation reports and 11 CO reports following accidents. All of the reports were from the period from 1997 to 2005, except one from 1990. The other reports from 1990 to 1996 were unavailable. The accidents had a mean estimated cost of 2,870,620 Norwegian krone (approximately $450,000). Each report was independently analyzed by the first and second authors, who had different backgrounds. The first author is an ergonomist, whereas the second author is a navigation instructor in the RNoN. The PSFs were classified according to a predefined criteria document. The criteria document was produced by the reviewers prior to the analysis, where detailed operational definitions for each PSF were stated. The definitions were adapted to the context of navigation, but based on the source methods. Because the PSFs were rarely clearly identified in the accident reports, they had to be largely inferred from the accident descriptions. For example, if the report stated that "at 4 a.m., the navigator had been on watch for 18 hours," this was considered a positive case of fatigue, time-of-day effects, and time on task. The operational definitions were "fatigue in one or more of the operators" (fatigue), "possible influence of time of day on operator performance" (time of day) and "one or more of the operators had continuously performed working tasks over an extended period of time." The definitions of the PSFs were based on those in the original taxonomy sources, but the identification of a PSF was based on our judgment of the factual information in the accident report.

The independent data sets were subsequently compared, and a consensus data set was made following discussion between the two reviewers. Each discrepancy was scrutinized in light of original report documents before consensus was reached. The interrater reliability for the PSFs between the two reviewers was low (Cohen's κ = .28). This could be due to issues such as low experience in PSF classification, inadequate PSF definitions, or the subjective nature of the accident reports.

Statistical Analyses

The final data set was analyzed using SPSS 12.0 software (SPSS Inc., 2003). Due to the small sample size and exploratory nature of this research, no inferential statistical analyses were possible. Descriptive analyses were performed on all background variables. Frequency data were then obtained for all PSF variables; variables with fewer than two cases were excluded from further analyses.

The remaining PSF variables were analyzed using binomial hierarchical cluster analysis (Everitt, 1993). The method works by hierarchically categorizing variables according to their similarity, based on the number of matching, positive cases. The optimal number of clusters was determined by finding the largest distance between cluster levels in the hierarchy. The purpose of performing the cluster analysis was to evaluate the presence of patterns in accident circumstances. Prior studies suggest that accidents may appear similar, yet have very different causes (Everitt, 1993). Thus, the purpose was to determine any natural PSF clusters in the accident data.

RESULTS

Background Factors

A majority (60%) of the vessels involved in the accidents had cruising speeds above 25 kt, and could be considered high-speed. Most of the accidents (94%) were groundings that did not lead to personal injury. Technical malfunctions were present in eight cases (23%); these included faulty rudders, depth finders, and navigational equipment. A majority of the cases (54%) occurred during training and evaluation. Accidents were evenly dispersed between light (40%) and dark (60%) seasons, weather conditions (76% in clear or overcast weather), and times of day (53% happened between 8 a.m. and 8 p.m.). Few accidents (16%) occurred in conditions with reduced visibility (i.e., rain or fog).

PSF Frequencies

Frequencies of the PSFs are shown in Figure 1. A total of 644 PSFs were identified in the review, with a mean of 18 PSFs per accident (range = 2–59, $SD = 12.8$). The most frequently occurring PSFs were operator expectations, high perceptual requirements, and attention. The majority of the PSFs were either related to human cognitive characteristics or cognitive task requirements. Around one quarter of the accidents involved PSFs related to work organization, such as team communication and distribution of workload. PSFs related to the man–machine interface and physical working conditions were generally uncommon.

Cluster Analysis

A hierarchical cluster analysis (within-group average linkage, Jaccard method) identified eight natural PSF clusters. These can be seen in Table 2, where the clusters are ranked according to the prevalence of the PSFs in them (sum in brackets).

The cluster sizes were exponentially distributed, as can be seen in Figure 2. This shows that there was a clear difference in the prevalence of the PSFs contained in the clusters, but also in size of the clusters. Demand–capability balance was clearly

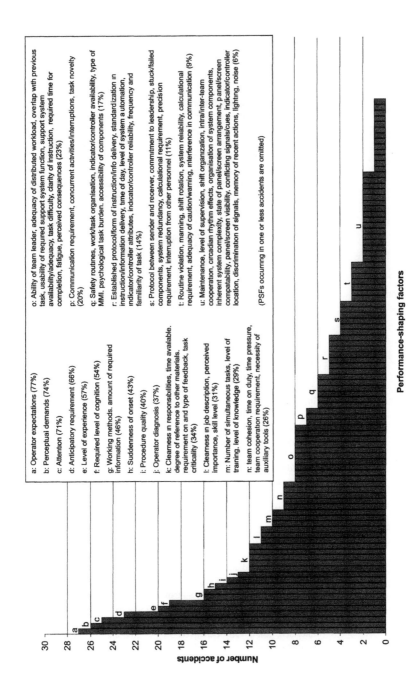

FIGURE 1 Frequency of performance-shaping factors identified in navigation accidents in the Royal Norwegian Navy from 1990 to 2005.

TABLE 2
Performance-Shaping Factor Clusters Identified in a Study of Navigation Accidents
in the Royal Norwegian Navy

Cluster Name	Variables in Cluster	Example
Demand-capability balance (n = 271)	Required time for completion, time available for operator performance, time pressure (time required vs. time available), knowledge level, attention, perceptual requirements, required level of cognition, operator expectations, anticipatory requirement, experience level, work methods, amount of required information, task criticality, requirement on and type of feedback, suddenness of onset, level of training, necessity of auxiliary tools, routine violations	*Fast patrol boat (FPB) grounding* An inexperienced navigator navigated the ship in difficult waters. After losing control over the exact position, he failed to observe a light and was late making a required turn. The vessel immediately ran into a submerged rock.
Work organization and distribution (n = 170)	Adequacy of distributed workload, intra/interteam cooperation, operator diagnosis, operator skill level, ability/leadership/authority of team leader, perceived importance, number of simultaneous goals/tasks, overlap with previous tasks, calculational requirement, clearness in job/role definition, clearness in responsibilities/communication lines, team cooperation requirement, communication requirement, clarity of instruction and terminology, procedure quality, concurrent activities and interruptions, degree of reference to other materials than procedures, shift rotation	*Collision between two FPBs* Two FPBs participating in an exercise were unaware of the other boat's position due to lack of radar and lantern use. The commanding officer (CO) knew the relative position of the boats, but failed to inform the navigator. The lookout (who was visually impaired) on one of the FPBs was unaware of the fact that he was on lookout duty, believing that his main task was to man one of the guns. The FPBs failed to see each other and collided.
Quality of bridge design (n = 61)	Interference in communication, indicator/controller attributes, interruption from other personnel, availability of indicators/controllers, availability/adequacy of support systems, usability of support system functions, physical accessibility of components, type of man–machine interface, task novelty, perceived consequences	*Coast guard vessel grounding* The sonar dome was left out by mistake following a crew change. The sonar indicator was only visible from one side of the bridge, leaving the navigator unaware of the ship's increased depth. The sonar dome was subsequently damaged when entering shallow waters.

(continued)

TABLE 2 (Continued)

Cluster Name	Variables in Cluster	Example
Fatigue, vigilance, and time of day effects ($n = 39$)	Fatigue, time on duty, psychological task burden, time of day, task difficulty, manning	*FPB grounding* A single FPB crew was ordered to sail during its planned rest period under an exercise in foreign waters The crew had been awake for almo 48 hr. The previous rest period was disturbed by high seas. The navigai misjudged two lights, and consequently ordered a wrong turn
Quality and reliability of system features ($n = 24$)	Adequacy of caution/warnings, level of system automation, indicator/controller reliability, stuck/failed components, system redundancy, system reliability	*Minesweeper grounding* The navigator ordered a turn using the autopilot system. When attempting to make a hard turn, the autopilot failed to turn at the programmed turn rate.
Quality of communication ($n = 15$)	Level of standardization in use of terminology, standardization in instruction/information delivery, protocol between sender and receiver, established protocol/form of instruction/information delivery	*Submarine grounding* A submarine CO issued an inappropriate order, which the helmsman carried out. The CO issued the helmsman a new order using nonstandard terminology. Th corrective order was misinterpretec by the helmsman, who carried it ou erroneously.
Unusual task issues ($n = 15$)	Frequency and familiarity of task, precision requirement, safety routines	*FPB grounding* An FPB was attempting to tow another FPB off ground. With no visual reference points and little maneuvering space, the assisting FPB drifted onto the ground.
Commitment to leadership ($n = 4$)	Commitment to leadership	

the largest cluster, consisting of 42% of the total PSFs. It consisted of PSFs related to the operator's cognitive characteristics, task requirements, and the operational system characteristics. Work organization and distribution was also large (27%), and mainly included PSFs related to team communication, workload distribution, and task organization. Quality of bridge design was a smaller cluster, and accounted for less than 10% of the total PSFs. The PSFs included in this category were generally related to problems with physical movement, system design, and communication problems. Fatigue, vigilance, and time-of-day effects accounted for 6% of the total, but also contained a low number of PSFs. These were related to

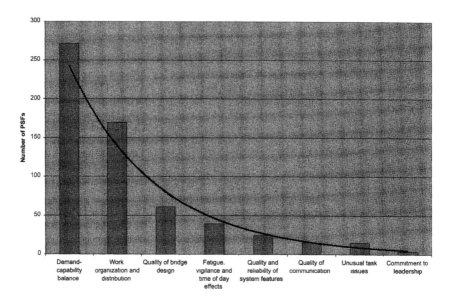

FIGURE 2   Cluster sizes ranked according to prevalence of performance-shaping factors (PSFs) identified.

issues with fatigue, task difficulty, and manning size. Quality and reliability of system features included 4% of the PSFs, and consisted of factors related to the technical system. Quality of communication and unusual task issues were equal in size, both accounting for 2%. Communication problems consisted of factors related to communication problems between crew members, whereas unusual task issues was made up of only three factors. Leadership problems consisted of only one (relatively rare) PSF: commitment to leadership. This PSF did not associate with any other factors, but was not alone or a salient feature in any of the accidents. No example has therefore been given for this cluster in Table 2.

DISCUSSION

PSFs

The results in our study show that navigation accidents in the RNoN are predominantly associated with PSFs related to the cognitive characteristics of the crew members and the sensory and cognitive requirements of the tasks performed. This supports the idea that navigation is an inherently difficult task (Hockey et al., 2003; Kjerstad, 2004) involving a high level of dynamism, complexity, and uncertainty (Norros, 2004). Our findings show that task requirements related to anticipation, perception, criticality, and diagnosis were among the most common PSFs found in the accidents. The difficulty of the task is also reflected in frequency of human-related PSFs found in the accidents, including level of experience, training, and attention.

What is it that makes navigation in the RNoN difficult? Our data show that neither adverse weather nor reduced visibility has been common at the time of the accidents, in contrast to the findings of LeBlanc and Rucks (1996). This could be explained on the basis of risk compensation, in that people will modify their behavior according to the level of risk to which they are exposed (Summala, 1996). The accidents also appeared to be distributed relatively evenly between different seasons and times of day. Faster vessel types were overrepresented compared to the slower ones, however, indicating that speeds often were high at the times of accidents. This is in concordance with the findings of Kjerstad (2004), who showed that increased speed positively influenced the risk of grounding. An important factor not covered by our data however, is the complexity of the waters in which the accidents have occurred (Cockroft, 1984). The environment can add to the uncertainty of navigation through the presence of invisible dangers (e.g., shallow waters and submerged rocks), but also through unpredictable behavior from other ships (Hockey et al., 2003).

In addition to uncertainty, dynamism and complexity are also important aspects of the difficulty in this type of navigation (Norros, 2004). Dynamism is reflected in that littoral navigation involves high time pressure, so operators are required to make quick (but important) decisions. Our findings showed that time-related PSFs such as suddenness of onset, time available, and task criticality all happened in more than one third of the accidents. This suggests that there is a difference between navigation on small naval vessels and large merchant ships, where monitoring constitutes a larger part of the task (Colquhoun et al., 1988).

The PSFs identified in our analysis also indicate a high level of complexity in the tasks preceding the accidents. More than one third of the accidents involved issues related to clearness in responsibilities and operator diagnosis, and more than half were related to the operator's required level of cognition. Lützhöft (2004) argued that navigating on modern ship bridges involves a high degree of integration work, where system performance is dependent on the effective division of tasks between multiple operators and increasingly advanced technology. This leads to the navigation task becoming complex, as it places demands on operator–operator interaction as well as operator–technology interaction.

Using cluster analysis, we were able to form a basis for a category structure of the PSFs. Our aim for doing this was to evaluate the presence of patterns for the PSFs, which could be helpful for building accident scenarios in the future. The results from the analysis showed that the accidents had distinctive characteristics, but also that some PSF categories were more important than others. The largest cluster (demand-capability balance) was comprised of PSFs related to task requirements and individual cognitive characteristics, which appeared to be the most significant PSF categories in the analysis. This was followed by the category work organization and distribution, which mainly consisted of factors related to teamwork and task organization. The smaller clusters were less prevalent, but could still have had a strong effect in the accidents in which they were involved. The relative number of PSFs related to the system and physical environment was considerably smaller than those related to the nature of the task itself. However, it is important to remember that cluster analysis does not evaluate strength of association, and cannot be used to make inferences because the results can only be generalized to the immediate sample (Everitt, 1993).

Methodological Limitations

A number of problems with bias arise when analyzing archival data, particularly regarding accidents (Drury, 1995). First, non-injury-producing accidents are underreported. Results from this study should therefore be limited to "worst-case" accidents. Second, the depth of inquiry is often proportionate to the severity of the accident. Background information is more detailed in cases where crew members were badly hurt. Third, accident reports are inherently biased by the competencies and concerns of the investigation committee members, leading to cases of differential misclassification. Reports are not standardized, and therefore tend to be heterogeneous. Investigators are often highly competent in the field of navigation, but not human factors, resulting in competence bias. As a result, conclusions have frequently taken the form of, for example, "the accident happened because of improper navigation conduct by the CO." The remedial action has accordingly been to instruct the CO to "follow established principles for safe navigation." For this reason, our analysis has not been focused on the conclusions in the reports, but rather the factual information on which they are based.

The low interrater reliability is problematic, but not crucial for the validity of our data. The subjective nature of many of the PSFs carries a high risk of inconsistent results, especially when based on secondary data sources such as accident reports written in natural language. This was particularly expected in this study, where the reports were evaluated by researchers with quite different backgrounds. We see the low level of agreement between the individual researchers as being somewhat less important, as the final data set was made through consensus. We believe that this approach strengthened the validity of our results by ensuring a more extensive, multidisciplinary data analysis.

Implications

Determining root causes of human error based on archival, retrospective data involves a high risk of bias, and is often inconsequential for improving safety

(Brown, 1995). However, Dekker (2002) stated that "human error is not random. It is systematically connected to features of people's tools, tasks and operating environment" (p. 61). This means that by improving knowledge of the PSFs that have been present in navigation accidents, we can better understand which measures may be suited for counteracting them. Second, and more important, PSF taxonomies also provide a basis for future research. For instance, the fidelity of simulator experiments could be improved by modeling high-risk scenarios on the most frequent PSFs found in this study. Finally, the results can be used to improve the reporting scheme for accidents in the navy and other maritime organizations.

Our findings showed that the most common PSFs associated with navigation accidents were related to task attributes and requirements and the cognitive characteristics of the operators. Because the operational characteristics of the system cannot be changed—the ships will only become faster—error must be reduced through other means. Reason (1990) suggested training as a potential measure, especially when directed toward improving fault diagnosis. Training operators to recognize potential system errors through the use of heuristics can improve their problem-solving skills when faced with high-risk situations. Simulator training is also proposed as a possible method for improving operator skills, but only if the simulation can effectively "recreate the dynamic and interactive nature of an accident sequence" (Reason, 1990, pp. 243–244).

CONCLUSIONS

Our study showed that a large number of PSFs were present in the navigation accident analyses. The most frequently occurring PSFs were related to operator expectations, perceptual demands, attention, anticipatory requirements, and level of experience. Cluster analyses showed that the PSFs could be naturally grouped into eight categories. Possible measures to improve safety and system performance include training, changing task organization, and improving bridge systems. More systematic data collection following mishaps is needed to provide a better understanding of naval navigation accidents.

REFERENCES

Brigham, F. R. (1972). Ergonomic problems in ship control. *Applied Ergonomics, 3,* 14–19.

Brown, I. D. (1995). Accident reporting and analysis. In J. R. Wilson & E. N. Corlett (Eds.), *Evaluation of human work* (2nd ed., pp. 969–992). London: Taylor & Francis.

Calvano, C., Byers, D., Harney, R., Papoulias, F., Markle H., Trevisan, R., et al. (2001). *"Sea Lance" littoral warfare small combatant system* (Rep. No. NPS-ME-01–001). Monterey, CA: Naval Postgraduate School.

Cockroft, A. N. (1984, June). Collisions at sea. *Safety at Sea,* pp. 17–19.

Colquhoun, W. P., Rutenfranz, J., Goethe, H., Neidhart, B., Condon, R., Plett, R., et al. (1988). Work at sea—A study of sleep, and of circadian-rhythms in physiological and psychological functions, in watchkeepers on merchant vessels: 1. Watchkeeping on board ships—A methodological approach. *International Archives of Occupational and Environmental Health, 60*, 321–329.

Dekker, S. (2002). *The field guide to human error investigations.* Aldershot, England: Ashgate.

Drury, C. D. (1995). The use of archival data. In J. R. Wilson & E. N. Corlett (Eds.), *Evaluation of human work* (2nd ed., pp. 101–112). London: Taylor & Francis.

Everitt, B. S. (1993). *Cluster analysis.* London: Arnold.

Farris, M. T., II, & Welch, D. (1998). High-speed ship technology: Maritime vessels for the 21st century. *Transportation Journal, 38*, 5.

Fuller, R., & Santos, J. A. (2002). *Human factors for highway engineers.* London: Pergamon.

Hockey, G. R. J., Healey, A., Crawshaw, M., Wastell, D. G., & Sauer, J. (2003). Cognitive demands of collision avoidance in simulated ship control. *Human Factors, 45*, 252–265.

Hollnagel, E. (1998). *Cognitive reliability and error analysis method.* Oxford, England: Elsevier Science.

Holton, C. (2003). New high tech, high-speed ship could rapidly deploy U.S. forces. *World Tribune.com.* Retrieved October 26, 2005, from http://216.26.163.62/2003/wtt_10_28.html

Johnson, C. W. (2000). Proving properties of accidents. *Reliability Engineering and System Safety, 67*, 175–191.

Kim, J. W., & Jung, W. D. (2003). A taxonomy of performance influencing factors for human reliability analysis of emergency tasks. *Journal of Loss Prevention in the Process Industries, 16*, 479–495.

Kirwan, B. (1998). Human error identification techniques for risk assessment of high-risk systems— Part 1: Review and evaluation of techniques. *Applied Ergonomics, 29*, 157–177.

Kjerstad, N. (2002, September). *Simulator for training and R&D in high-speed navigation.* Paper presented at the International MARTECH-2002 conference, Singapore Maritime Academy and Maritime and Port Authorities of Singapore, Singapore.

Kjerstad, N. (2004, April). *Navigators' response to critical information: Testing with state-of-the-art high-speed craft cockpit simulator.* Paper presented at the International Conference on Navigation in Channels and Restricted Waters, the Arab Institute of Navigation, Cairo, Egypt.

LeBlanc, L. A., & Rucks, C. T. (1996). A multiple discriminant analysis of vessel accidents. *Accident Analysis and Prevention, 28*, 501–510.

Lützhöft, M. (2004). *"The technology is great when it works": Maritime technology and human integration on the ship's bridge.* Unpublished doctoral dissertation, University of Linköping, Linköping, Sweden.

Mulcahy, F. S. (2005). High-speed sealift is a joint mission. *Proceedings of the U.S. Naval Institute, 131*, 34–37.

The Nautical Institute. (2003, October). Just waiting to happen ... The work of the UK P&I Club. *Alert! The International Maritime Human Element Bulletin*, pp. 1, 3.

Norros, L. (2004). *Acting under uncertainty.* Espoo, Finland: VTT Publications.

Norwegian Ministry of Defence. (2005). *Accident report archive.* Oslo, Norway: Author.

Reason, J. (1990). *Human error.* Cambridge, England: Cambridge University Press.

Sarter, N. B., & Amalberti, R. (2000). *Cognitive engineering in the aviation domain.* Mahwah, NJ: Lawrence Erlbaum Associates, Inc.

Sasou, K., & Reason, J. (1999). Team errors: Definition and taxonomy. *Reliability Engineering and System Safety, 65*, 1–9.

SPSS, Inc. (2003). SPSS (Version 12.0) [Computer software]. Chicago: Author.

Summala, H. (1996). Accident risk and driver behaviour. *Safety Science, 22*, 103–117.

Swain, A. D., & Guttman, H. E. (1983). *Handbook of human reliability analysis with emphasis on nuclear power plant applications* (NUREG/CR 1278 ed.). Albuquerque, NM: Sandia National Laboratories.

Wagenaar, W. A., & Groeneweg, J. (1987). Accidents at sea: Multiple causes and impossible conse-quences. *International Journal of Man–Machine Studies, 27,* 587–598.

Whalley, S. P. (1988). Minimising the cause of human error. In G. P. Libberton (Ed.), *10th Advances in Reliability Technology Symposium: University of Bradford.* New York: Elsevier.

Wilson, J. R., Cordiner, L., Nichols, S., Norton, L., Bristol, N., Clarke, T., et al. (2001). On the right track: Systematic implementation of ergonomics in railway network control. *Cognition, Technology & Work, 3,* 238–252.

Yacavone, D. W. (1993). Mishap trends and cause factors in naval aviation—A review of Naval Safety Center data, 1986–90. *Aviation, Space, and Environmental Medicine, 64,* 392–395.

MILITARY PSYCHOLOGY, 2006, *18*(Suppl.), S131–S148

Resilience Under Military Operational Stress: Can Leaders Influence Hardiness?

Paul T. Bartone

Industrial College of the Armed Forces
National Defense University

Although many people suffer physical and mental health decrements following exposure to stress, many others show remarkable resilience, remaining healthy despite high stress levels. If the factors that account for resilience can be clearly identified and understood, perhaps resilience can be enhanced even for those most vulnerable to stress. One potential pathway to resilience is personality hardiness, a characteristic sense that life is meaningful, we choose our own futures, and change is interesting and valuable. This article applies this hardiness concept to the context of military operational stress, and argues that highly effective leaders can increase hardy, resilient responses to stressful circumstances within their units. I discuss the nature of stress in modern military operations, and briefly review relevant hardiness theory and research. Three sets of considerations lead to the proposition that hardy leaders can indeed increase hardy cognitions and behaviors in groups. These considerations concern (a) the likely underlying mechanisms of hardiness, which have to do with how experiences get interpreted and made sense of; (b) relevant theoretical positions on leader social influence, including transformational leadership and path–goal leader theory; and (c) several empirical studies that have shown indirect support for a hardy leader influence process. A case vignette is provided to illustrate how leaders might increase hardy cognitions, attitudes, and behaviors within their organizations during highly stressful operations. This potential for leaders to boost hardiness as a pathway to resiliency in groups under stress merits further active investigation.

Military operations across the entire range of conflict expose military personnel (and increasingly, contract workers) to a multitude of stressors. These stressors can lead to a variety of negative health consequences, both physical and mental, for

Correspondence should be addressed to Paul T. Bartone, Colonel, U.S. Army, Professor of Behavioral Sciences, Industrial College of the Armed Forces, National Defense University, Ft. McNair, Washington, DC 20319–5062. E-mail: bartonep@ndu.edu

some exposed individuals. For example, Hoge et al. (2004) recently reported that up to 17% of U.S. veterans of the Iraq conflict reported symptoms of major depression, anxiety, or posttraumatic stress disorder (PTSD). However, a point that is often neglected in studies of this kind is that most exposed individuals appear to respond with remarkable resiliency to stress, and this includes very severe or traumatic stress (Bonanno, 2004). For example, most survivors of the September 11, 2001, attack on the Pentagon appear to have adjusted extremely well to this acutely stressful event, with no formal mental health intervention other than practical support provided in the aftermath (Ritchie, Leavitt, & Hanish, 2006). Similarly, as pointed out by Wessely (2005), the vast majority of Londoners responded to the July 2005 terrorist strikes on the London public transit system not with psychopathology, but with resilience. One examination of historical events during World War II also shows the same pattern of broad public resilience, rather than breakdown in the face of the Nazi German bombings of London that killed 40,000 people (Jones, Woolven, Durodie, & Wessely, 2004).

What accounts for such resiliency? If the factors or pathways that lead to human resiliency under stress were better understood, perhaps some of these resiliency factors could be developed or amplified in those who are initially low in resilience, and more vulnerable to stress. Such an approach now seems even more important, given the generally recognized failure of postdisaster psychological interventions such as critical incident stress debriefing (Mitchell & Everly, 2000) to make any positive difference for those receiving them (van Emmerik, Kamphuis, Hulsbosch, & Emmelkamp, 2002). Worse, in many cases such interventions appear to increase rather than decrease the incidence of later psychological problems (Wessely, 2005). This article focuses attention on personality hardiness, one of several potential "pathways to resilience" posited by Bonanno (2004). Based on both theoretical and empirical grounds, I argue that leaders in military units may well be able to foster increases in the kinds of cognitions and behaviors that typify the high-hardy person's response to stressful circumstances.

It is useful to begin by describing the nature of the stressors encountered by troops in modern military operations. Following this, the hardiness construct is explained in some detail, including both theoretical background and some empirical findings showing that hardiness serves to buffer or moderate the ill effects of stress. I suggest that the primary underlying mechanism in the hardiness–resiliency process involves how stressful experiences get interpreted or made sense of in the context of one's entire life experience. Several theoretical positions support the view that leaders may influence this process in work groups such as military units. High-hardy leaders may facilitate positive coping with stress by shaping the shared understandings of stressful events and experiences within the group in a positive and constructive direction. Although this stands now as a theoretical proposition for future research to evaluate more fully, several studies already provide indirect support for this hardy leader influence process. To clarify how this process might occur in military groups, a brief case report is presented of a U.S. Army unit deployed to the Middle East.

THE NATURE OF STRESSORS IN MODERN MILITARY OPERATIONS

Military operations always entail stressors of various kinds for the troops involved. Historically, the extreme stressors of combat and all-out war have received the greatest attention. However, military operations in the post-Cold War era bring additional challenges and stressors. For one thing, as the number of peacekeeping, peacemaking, humanitarian, and other kinds of operations increases, while military organizations shrink in size with the shift to all-volunteer forces, units are deploying more frequently. Increased deployments entail other stressful changes in military units as well, such as an increased number (and intensity) of training exercises, planning sessions, and equipment inspections, all of which increase the workload and pace of operations (Castro & Adler, 1999). Furthermore, more frequent deployments also involve more family separations, a recognized stressor for soldiers (Bell, Bartone, Bartone, Schumm, & Gade, 1997).

One obvious way to reduce the stress associated with military operations is to lessen the frequency and duration of deployments. Although this may be a sensible policy approach in principle, it is not always possible given political and strategic realities and limited resources. The same is true in other occupations and contexts. For example, following the September 11th terrorist strike on the World Trade Center, fire, police, and other emergency personnel necessarily maintained continuous operations around the clock with the goal of locating possible survivors, as well as restoring essential services to the affected areas. As this is written, thousands of disaster response workers are currently working to rescue victims and restore basic services in New Orleans and surrounding areas ravaged by Hurricane Katrina in August 2005. In situations such as this, continuous operations and extreme efforts are necessary to save lives; easing the pace of work is generally seen as an unacceptable (if not unethical) compromise. So, when reducing stressful operations or activities is not an option, what can be done to minimize or counter the stressors associated with such operations? In particular, is there anything that leaders can do to facilitate healthy coping with operational stress? To answer this question with respect to the military case, it helps to have a clearer understanding of the nature of the stressors encountered by soldiers on modern military deployments. What is it about modern military deployments that is stressful for those performing them? Extensive field research with U.S. military units deployed to Croatia, Bosnia, Kuwait, and Saudi Arabia from 1993 through 1996, including interviews, observations, and survey data, aimed to identify the primary sources of stress for soldiers on operations. This work led to the identification of five primary psychological stress dimensions in modern military operations (Bartone, 2001; Bartone, Adler, & Vaitkus, 1998). These are isolation, ambiguity, powerlessness, boredom, and danger. Today, the increased frequency and pace of deployments for U.S. forces and the long work hours and days that these deployments entail (Castro & Adler, 1999) merit the inclusion of another factor, probably best described as workload or deployment stress. These dimensions are summarized in Table 1 and further elaborated next.

TABLE 1
Primary Stressor Dimensions in Modern Military Operations

Stressor	Characteristics
1. Isolation	Remote location Foreign culture and language Distant from family and friends Unreliable communication tools Newly configured units, do not know your coworkers
2. Ambiguity	Unclear mission or changing mission Unclear rules of engagement Unclear command or leadership structure Role confusion (what is my job?) Unclear norms or standards of behavior (what is acceptable here and what is not?)
3. Powerlessness	Movement restrictions Rules of engagement constraints on response options Policies prevent intervening, providing help Forced separation from local culture, people, events, and places Unresponsive supply chain—trouble getting needed supplies and repair parts Differing standards of pay, movement, behavior, etc., for different units in area Indeterminate deployment length—do not know when we are going home Do not know or cannot influence what is happening with family back home
4. Boredom (alienation)	Long periods of repetitive work activities without variety Lack of work that can be construed as meaningful or important Overall mission or purpose not understood as worthwhile or important Few options for play and entertainment
5. Danger (threat)	Real risk of serious injury or death, from: Enemy fire, bullets, mortars, mines, explosive devices, etc. Accidents, including "friendly fire" Disease, infection, toxins in the environment Chemical, biological, or nuclear materials used as weapons
6. Workload	High frequency, duration, and pace of deployments Long work hours and/or days during the deployments Long work hours and/or days in periods before and after deployments

Isolation

Soldiers deploy to remote locations, far away from home, separated from their families, frequently without good tools or methods for communicating. They find themselves in a strange land and culture, often surrounded by coworkers who are new to them, as the deployed unit was specially configured for a particular mission. They feel isolated and alone.

Ambiguity

Often in modern military operations, the mission and rules of engagement are unclear, there are multiple missions that are in conflict, or the mission changes over time. The role and purpose of the soldier may be similarly unclear. Confusion and mystery in the command structure adds to this uncertainty (who is in charge of what?). Lack of understanding of host nation language and cultural practices, and how these impact on deployed forces, further adds to the uncertainty (which norms and practices are acceptable in the host culture, and which are not?). This uncertainty can also pertain to other national contingents in a multinational coalition force.

Powerlessness

Security and operational concerns (e.g., "force protection") often lead to movement restrictions; for example, soldiers are not allowed to leave their base camp. Soldiers may also be unable to interact with the local populace, and are prevented from doing the things they are used to doing (e.g., running or jogging for exercise, displaying their home country's flag), and may also face a variety of restrictions on dress and behavior. They have few choices. Movement and communication restrictions also prevent soldiers from learning about local culture and language, and resources that might be available locally, adding to their sense of powerlessness. They may also observe soldiers from other branches or national contingents operating with different rules and privileges in the same environment, but have no explanation for these different standards. And soldiers may see local people in need of help—wounded, ill, hungry, or despairing—but be unable to give assistance due to movement and contact rules and regulations.[1]

Boredom

Modern military missions frequently involve long periods of "staying in place," often without significant work to do. As the weeks and months tick by, soldiers start

---

[1]Others have noted the significance of a sense of powerlessness in peacekeeping operations. For example, Weisaeth and Sund (1982) found that in Norwegian soldiers serving in Lebanon under the UNIFIL United Nations peacekeeping mission, the feeling of being powerless to act or intervene was a main contributor to posttraumatic stress symptoms.

to get bored. To some degree, this can be countered by providing more entertainment and sports activities for soldiers. However, the real problem of boredom seems to result from lack of meaningful work or constructive activities in which to engage. Daily tasks often take on a repetitive dullness, with a sense that nothing important is being accomplished.

Danger

This dimension encompasses the real physical dangers and threats that are often present in the deployed environment, threats that can result in injury or death. Things like bullets, mines, bombs, or other hazards in the deployed setting are included here, as well as the risk of accidents, disease, and exposure to toxic substances. In current U.S. and coalition operations in Iraq and Afghanistan, this includes many hidden dangers such as suicide bombers, snipers, and improvised explosive devices (IEDs). This source of stress can be direct, representing threats to oneself, or indirect, representing threats to one's comrades. Exposure to severely injured or dead people, and the psychological stress this can entail, is also considered under this stress dimension.

Workload

This factor represents the increasing frequency, length, and rapid pace of deployments that many military units are encountering. Also, most deployments are characterized by a 24-hr, 7-day-a-week work schedule in which soldiers are always on duty, with no time off. Work-related sleep deprivation is often a related feature. Training and preparation activities in the period leading up to a deployment also usually entail a heavy workload and extremely long days. The same is generally true for military units returning home from a deployment, who must work overtime to assure that all vehicles and equipment are properly cleaned, maintained, and accounted for.

It is important to remember that although these major dimensions of stress on modern military operations are discussed as six distinct factors, in practice they overlap and interact in multiple ways (Bartone, 2001; Bartone et al., 1998). The next question is what tools, strategies, or coping mechanisms can be applied to increase resiliency or resistance to these stressors, both at the individual and unit levels. Some authors have suggested that unit cohesion is a powerful influence on unit resiliency under stress (Ingraham & Manning, 1981; Paton, 1997), and that leadership can also play an important role (Kirkland, Bartone, & Marlowe, 1993; Watson, Ritchie, Demer, Bartone, & Pfefferbaum, 2006). In what follows I focus attention on the personality dimension of hardiness, and suggest how leaders might utilize this construct to increase individual and group resiliency under stress.

PERSONALITY HARDINESS

In considering the question of what leaders can do to facilitate healthy coping with the stress of military operations, it is useful to take a closer look at what hardiness is, and consider how it might operate as a stress resiliency factor. Conceptually, hardiness is a personality dimension that develops early in life and is reasonably stable over time, although amenable to change and probably trainable under certain conditions (Kobasa, 1979; Maddi & Kobasa, 1984). Hardy persons have a high sense of life and work commitment, a greater feeling of control, and are more open to change and challenges in life. They tend to interpret stressful and painful experiences as a normal aspect of existence, part of life that is overall interesting and worthwhile.

The concept of hardiness is not new. It is theoretically grounded in the work of existential philosophers and psychologists such as Heidegger (1986), Frankl (1960), and Binswanger (1963), and involves the creation of meaning in life, even life that is sometimes painful or absurd, and having the courage to live life fully despite its inherent pain and futility. It is a global perspective that affects how one views the self, others, work, and even the physical world (in existential terms, *Umwelt,* the "around" or physical world; *Mitwelt,* the "with" or social world; and *Eigenwelt,* the world of the self or me). As early as 1967, using somewhat different terms, Maddi outlined the hardy personality type and contrasted it with the nonhardy "existential neurotic." He used the term *ideal identity* to describe the person who lives a vigorous and proactive life, with an abiding sense of meaning and purpose, and a belief in his own ability to influence things.

Since Kobasa's (1979) original report on hardiness and health in executives, an extensive body of research has accumulated showing that hardiness protects against the ill effects of stress on health and performance. Studies with a variety of occupational groups have found that hardiness operates as a significant moderator or buffer of stress (e.g., Bartone, 1989; Contrada, 1989; Kobasa, Maddi, & Kahn, 1982; Roth, Wiebe, Fillingim, & Shay, 1989; Wiebe, 1991). Hardiness has also been identified as a moderator of combat exposure stress in Gulf War soldiers (Bartone, 1993, 1999a, 2000). Personality hardiness has emerged as a stress buffer in other military groups as well, including U.S. Army casualty assistance workers (Bartone, Ursano, Wright, & Ingraham, 1989), peacekeeping soldiers (Bartone, 1996; Britt, Adler, & Bartone, 2001), Israeli soldiers in combat training (Florian, Mikulincer, & Taubman, 1995), Israeli officer candidates (Westman, 1990), and Norwegian Navy cadets (Bartone, Johnsen, Eid, Brun, & Laberg, 2002).

Figure 1 shows results from a study on hardiness, combat stress, and PTSD symptoms in U.S. active duty soldiers who fought in the Gulf War (Bartone, 2000). This figure shows the typical, and rather robust interaction of hardiness and stress, wherein it is under high-stress conditions that the resiliency effects of hardiness are most apparent. In this study, high-hardy U.S. Army soldiers exposed to combat

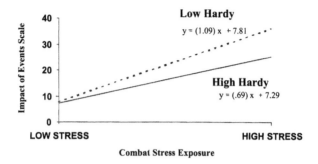

FIGURE 1   Gulf War combat stress exposure predicting Impact of Events Scale scores for low and high hardy groups, active duty sample. Displays Hardy × Combat Stress Exposure interaction ($p < .0001$) in regression model. $N = 824$ active duty, unstandardized betas used to map regression lines. Reprinted from Bartone (2000). Used with permission.

stress in the Gulf War showed significantly fewer traumatic stress symptoms (as assessed by the Impact of Events Scale; Horowitz, Wilner, & Alvarez, 1979).

PERSONALITY HARDINESS AS A FRAMEWORK FOR UNDERSTANDING POSITIVE LEADER INFLUENCE

How does hardiness operate to increase resiliency to stress? Although the underlying processes are still not clear, a critical aspect of the hardiness resiliency mechanism likely involves the interpretation, or the meaning that people attach to events around them and their own place in this world of experiences. High-hardy people typically interpret experience as (a) overall interesting and worthwhile; (b) something they can exert control over; and (c) challenging, presenting opportunities to learn and grow. It seems likely that in organized work groups such as the military, this meaning-making process is something that leaders can have considerable influence over. Military units by their nature are group oriented and highly interdependent. The typical tasks and missions are group ones, and the hierarchical authority structure frequently puts leaders in a position to exercise substantial control and influence over subordinates. By the policies and priorities they establish, the directives they give, the advice and counsel they offer, the stories they tell, and perhaps most important the examples they provide, leaders may indeed alter the manner in which their subordinates interpret and make sense of their experiences. Some empirical support for this notion comes from a study by Britt et al. (2001), who found (using structural equation modeling) that hardiness increases the perception of meaningful work, which in turn increases the perception of positive benefits associated with a stressful military deployment to Bosnia.

Many authors have commented on how social processes can influence the creation of meaning by individuals. Notable examples include Berger and Luckmann (1966) on the social construction of reality, Janis (1982) on groupthink, and Weik (1995) on the process of sensemaking in organizations. Even Allport (1985), the distinguished American personality psychologist, viewed individual meaning as often largely the result of social influence processes. It would seem that peers, leaders, indeed the entire unit or organizational culture can influence how experiences get interpreted. This leads to what we can term the *hardy leader influence hypothesis:* Leaders who are high in hardiness themselves exert influence on their subordinates to interpret stressful experiences in ways characteristic of high-hardy persons.

RESEARCH SUPPORTING THE HARDY LEADER INFLUENCE HYPOTHESIS

Data from several studies with cadets in training to be military officers lend support to the notion that leaders high in hardiness may influence subordinates to think and behave in more hardy or resilient ways. To measure hardiness, these studies used a 15-item scale that (a) includes both positively and negatively keyed items; (b) covers the three hardiness facets of commitment, control, and challenge; and (c) shows excellent validity and reliability (Bartone, 1995, 2000; Bartone & Snook, 2000). This measure is a shortened version of the Dispositional Resilience Scale (DRS; Bartone et al., 1989) identified by Funk (1992) in his review of hardiness theory and research as the best available tool for assessing hardiness. Also using the DRS hardiness measure, Sinclair and Tetrick (2000) found that hardiness operates independently of neuroticism (Funk & Houston, 1987), and that the theoretical structure of three facets (commitment, control, and challenge) nested beneath a superordinate hardiness construct is supported by confirmatory factor analysis.

In the first cadet study, the short hardiness scale was administered to a single West Point cohort ($N = 435$) during spring of their senior (fourth and final) year at the academy. Leader performance was assessed with military development (MD) grades, which are assigned to cadets at the end of each academic semester at West Point. These grades represent an average of leader performance ratings given by an officer supervisor, and the ratings of two or three cadet (upperclassmen) supervisors (U.S. Corps of Cadets, 1995). Multiple regression analysis predicting cumulative MD grades across 4 years (multiple $R = .23$), $F(8, 1141) = 11.95$, $p < .001$, identified hardiness, transformational leadership style (Bass, 1998), and several other variables as significant independent predictors of leader performance (Bartone, 1999b; Milan, Bourne, Zazanis, & Bartone, 2002). Personality hardiness emerged as the strongest and most consistent predictor of military development

TABLE 2
Leadership (Military Development) Predictors, West Point, 4 Years Total

Predictor	β	T	p
Hardiness	.15	5.1	< .00
Transformational leadership	.11	3.9	< .00
College entrance scores	.07	2.5	< .01
Social judgment	.07	2.3	< .02
Emotional stability	−.07	−2.2	< .03
Extraversion	.07	2.0	< .04
Traditional values	.07	2.0	< .04

Note. From Bartone (1999b). Multiple regression, backward elimination, mean substitution for missing data. Model: $F(8, 1141) = 11.95$, $p < .0001$. Multiple $R = .23$.

grades for these officer cadets (Table 2). In a similar study, hardiness proved to be an even stronger predictor of leader performance for women cadets, as compared to men (Bartone & Snook, 2000). These studies show that cadets who are high in hardiness perform more effectively as leaders, as indicated by external ratings of cadet peers and faculty supervisors. This does not indicate that they are influencing hardiness levels in their subordinates. However, it does show that cadets high in hardiness are rated more favorably on the various criteria included in the definition of effective leadership at West Point. In particular, it shows that they are admired by their subordinates. This provides a necessary (if not sufficient) condition for the hardy leader social influence process posited here.

In these cadet data, transformational leadership style (Bass, 1998; Burns, 1978) also predicts leadership performance in cadets, although not as strongly as hardiness. A subsequent correlational analysis revealed that transformational leadership is not significantly correlated with hardiness, although transformational leadership is moderately correlated with the hardiness facet of commitment. It is possible that those high in personality hardiness are more apt to develop a transformational leadership style, but that this occurs only under certain environmental or organizational conditions. This is an important question for future research to address.

Together these results indicate that Army cadets who are higher in hardiness—a characteristic sense of commitment, control, and challenge—are more effective as leaders in a military-type organization. Again, this shows that such leaders have the esteem of their subordinates, which may be a necessary precondition for hardy leader social influence to occur. To the extent that leader performance ratings also reflect performance of the groups being led, and that group performance is at least partly a function of effective coping with stress, these results also lend indirect support to the hardy leader social influence process. This is to say that the high-hardy cadet is rated as a better leader in part because he or she has aided the group to adjust and perform well under stressful conditions.

Another study done with Norwegian Navy officer cadets also supports a hardy leader effect on groups. This study sought to identify factors that contribute to developing cohesion in squad-sized units undergoing an intense 2-week training exercise (Bartone et al., 2002). Results showed that hardiness and small unit leadership influenced cohesion levels in a positive direction, and that hardiness and leadership interacted to influence cohesion. This suggests that what leaders do, and how they are perceived by their subordinates, can have a team-building or cohesion-enhancing effect on the unit. An additional finding, that personality hardiness is also associated with higher cohesion levels in the wake of a stressful group experience, further suggests a sense-making mechanism for such leader effects.

The key operative power of hardiness to buffer or transform stressful experiences seems to be related to the particular interpretations of such experiences that are typically made by the hardy person. If a stressful or painful experience can be cognitively framed and made sense of within a broader perspective that holds that all of existence is essentially interesting, worthwhile, fun, a matter of personal choice, and providing chances to learn and grow, then the stressful experience can have beneficial psychological effects instead of harmful ones. In a small group context, leaders are in a unique position to shape how stressful experiences are understood by members of the group. The leader who, through example and discussion, communicates a positive construction or reconstruction of shared stressful experiences, may exert an influence on the entire group in the direction of his or her interpretation of experience. Thus, leaders who are high in hardiness likely have a greater impact in their groups under high-stress conditions, when by their example, as well as by the explanations they give to the group, they encourage others to interpret stressful events as interesting challenges that they are capable of meeting, and in any case can learn and benefit from. This process itself, as well as the positive result (a shared understanding of the stressful event as something worthwhile and beneficial) could also be expected to generate an increased sense of shared values, mutual respect, and cohesion. Further support for this interpretation comes from the regression results showing that hardiness and leadership interact to affect postexercise cohesion levels (Bartone et al., 2002). This interaction effect means that the positive influence of leaders on the growth of unit cohesion is greater when hardiness levels in the unit are high to begin with. Once again, this does not confirm a direct influence of leaders on the hardiness levels of subordinates; however, it does suggest that leaders can influence positive interpretations of stressful events within a group, and that hardiness plays a role in this process.

Several theoretical ideas from the leadership literature are also relevant to the hardy leader influence process postulated here. In a thoughtful essay on the psychology of military leadership, Gal (1987) argued that for future and more demanding military operations, military leaders are needed who can increase the commitment of subordinates. According to Gal, this is the central operative activity of transformational leaders; that is, to increase the overall commitment levels of subordinates. The research on hardiness and leader performance summarized earlier suggests that leaders who are high in hardiness may be especially skilled at building up this sense of commitment in subordinates, and further suggests that how experiences get interpreted (interpretations shaped by leaders) is a critical part of the process.

Another relevant leadership theory is generally referred to as transformational leadership (Bass, 1998; Burns, 1978). As elaborated by Bass (1998), transformational leadership goes beyond reward and punishment approaches, and inspires subordinates to higher levels of effort and commitment. Conceptually, it includes the four elements of idealized influence, inspirational motivation, individualized consideration, and intellectual stimulation (Bass & Avolio, 1994). The transformational leader dimension of inspirational motivation is one of special relevance to the question of how hardy leaders might influence others in a work group. Bass and Avolio described inspirational motivation as follows:

> Transformational leaders behave in ways that motivate and inspire those around them by providing meaning and challenge to their followers' work. Team spirit is aroused. Enthusiasm and optimism are displayed. The leader gets followers involved in envisioning attractive future states. The leader clearly communicates expectations that followers want to meet and also demonstrates commitment to goals and the shared vision. (p. 3)

This description makes it clear that transformational leadership is believed to work in part through some process whereby leaders generate an increased sense of meaning, commitment, and challenge among their subordinates. The process itself is not further elaborated by transformational leadership theorists. The hardy leader influence hypothesis presented here suggests a possible mechanism underlying the inspirational motivation aspect of transformational leadership.

Increasing commitment and motivation is also an important feature of path–goal leadership theory, which focuses attention on how leaders influence the motivation of subordinates by identifying significant goals, structuring situations so that subordinates experience personal rewards for goal attainment, and clarifying the pathways for achieving these desired goals (House, 1971, 1996). According to path–goal theory, leaders may demonstrate supportive, directive, participative, or achievement leadership depending on their personal style and preference, as well as the contingencies of particular situations or tasks (House & Mitchell, 1974). Most relevant to the hardy leader influence hypothesis is the achievement leadership orientation of path–goal theory. This leader is somehow able to tap into and even increase followers' motivation to surmount obstacles and achieve goals, and to orient this achievement motivation toward important group goals. This is very similar to what the high-hardy person does at the individual level when confronted with unexpected or highly stressful situations; he or she tends to interpret these situations as challenges to meet head-on, to learn and grow from, rather than as threats or disruptions to be avoided. Path–goal leadership theory thus provides a broader framework for understanding how high-hardy leaders might influence the motivation, thinking, and behavior of subordinates.

CASE STUDY: HOW A HARDY LEADER CAN INFLUENCE GROUP HARDINESS ON MILITARY OPERATIONS

The following case vignette is provided to illustrate how the hardy leader influence process might operate in a deployed military unit. The case is a real one, identified during research conducted in 1995 with a U.S. Army unit deployed to Saudi Arabia as part of a deterrent or peace enforcement operation. I had the opportunity to visit this unit as part of a study of deployment stress, morale, and cohesion in U.S. Army Air Defense Artillery (ADA) battalions. After the Gulf War ended in 1991, ADA battalions were stationed in Saudi Arabia and Kuwait to guard against possible Iraqi missile attacks. Units deployed for about 6 months, and then were replaced by other ADA units.

The unit under study was about 4.5 months into the mission, and things had by this time become dull and predictable for the soldiers. As the research team conducted interviews and surveys throughout the battalion, it became clear that unit morale was extremely low, as was cohesion in all the batteries or companies examined. However, morale and cohesion levels were dramatically different in one part of the battalion: the headquarters and maintenance company. Here, morale was high and cohesion was strong, in dramatic contrast to the other elements of the battalion. How could this difference be understood?

The company commander provided a ready explanation for his unit's high morale and cohesion. As he told it, shortly after they arrived in theater he put the company to work on a major task that provided a common goal, and a tangible mission to work on during their 6 months in the desert. He had heard about a nearby area that had been used as an equipment dump after the Gulf War. Tons of old military equipment and parts were buried in the sand, rusted, and dirty. The commander decided to assign his unit the task of excavating this area, and recovering, cleaning, and repairing as much equipment as possible over the course of their deployment. By the final stage of their 6-month rotation, they had salvaged over $1 million worth of equipment from the dump, and returned it to the Army supply system in good working order. The walls of their company work area and meeting room were bedecked with photographs showing before-and-after scenes of the equipment dump. Adding to the sense of accomplishment and transformation, the soldiers had built a multipurpose athletic field on the former dump site, which the entire battalion was using for sports events. Regardless of rank, all unit members spoke with great pride about this accomplishment.

This small example shows how a proactive, committed, high-hardy leader might influence an entire work group in the direction of greater hardiness and stress resiliency. The company commander took creative control of an ambiguous situation, and proceeded to define a meaningful mission for his unit. He essentially created a major task, something that was challenging, that he and his troops could exercise control over; then he helped his soldiers develop a shared sense of commitment to the task. It is also noteworthy that the task he generated had a clear goal or end state that could be accomplished with the available resources and time. He got his soldiers and subordinate leaders involved in the planning and execution, and led by example throughout. This leader also knew how to capitalize on recognition and pride in accomplishment, posting pictures and progress reports, and arranging for outside recognition from senior leaders and national news media. This external recognition further contributed to an enhanced sense of positive meaning within the work group, and a shared belief that what they had done was important and valuable. Whereas other units in the same battalion languished in alienation, boredom, and powerlessness, under the same external stressful conditions this one leader was able to increase unit morale and cohesion, commitment, control, and challenge within his company. This example suggests how a high-hardy leader may be able to influence his or her entire unit toward more hardy interpretations of experience, and the positive, resilient reactions that can follow.

CONCLUSIONS

As we have seen, several theoretical formulations as well as a number of research studies lend support to the hypothesis that hardy leaders can generate increasingly "hardy" and positive shared interpretations of experience, at least in the context of highly demanding military training activities and exercises. Can this valuable leader influence apply in other circumstances as well, such as mass casualties or disasters, or modern military deployments that entail the kinds of psychological stressors outlined earlier?

Although more focused research is certainly needed to answer this question definitively, there is now sufficient evidence to justify a qualified affirmative, and to provide a preliminary profile of how the high-hardy leader behaves to influence hardiness and stress resilience in an entire unit. The prototypical hardy leader leads by example, providing subordinates with a role model of the hardy approach to life, work, and reactions to stressful experiences. Through actions and words, he or she demonstrates a strong sense of commitment, control, and challenge, and a way of responding to stressful circumstances that demonstrates stress can be valuable, and that stressful events always at least provide the opportunity to learn and grow. A hardy leader facilitates "hardy" group sense-making of experience, in how tasks or missions are planned, discussed, and executed, and also as to how mistakes, failures, and casualties are spoken about and interpreted. Although most of this sense-making influence occurs through normal day-to-day interactions and communications, occasionally it can happen in the context of more formal after-action reviews, or debriefings that can focus attention on events as learning opportunities and create shared positive constructions of events and responses around events.[2] A hardy leader also seeks out (or creates if necessary) meaningful and challenging group tasks, and then capitalizes on group accomplishments by providing recognition, awards, and opportunities to reflect on and magnify positive results (e.g., photographs, news accounts, and other tangible mementos).

In work groups such as the military, where individuals are regularly exposed to extreme work-related stressors and hazards, leaders are in a unique position to shape how stressful experiences are made sense of, interpreted, and understood by members of the group. The leader who by example, discussion, and policies communicates a positive construction or reconstruction of shared stressful experiences, may exert an influence on the entire group in the direction of his or her interpretation of experience—toward more resilient and hardy sense making. Given the promising results seen thus far, this hardy leader influence process merits further active empirical investigation. A better knowledge and understanding of the processes underlying resilience would be of substantial value not just for military organizations, but for anyone interested in promoting resiliency and health in groups exposed to highly stressful circumstances.

ACNOWLEDGMENTS

Portions of this article appeared in Bartone, P. T. (2004). Increasing resiliency through shared sensemaking: Building hardiness in groups. In D. Paton, J. M. Violanti, C. Dunning, & L. M. Smith (Eds.), *Managing traumatic stress risk: A proactive approach* (pp. 129–140). Springfield, IL: Thomas.

---

[2]A recent National Institute of Mental Health (2002) report on best practices for early psychological interventions following mass violence events noted great confusion regarding the term *debriefing*. The authors recommend that the term be reserved for operational after-action reviews, and not be applied to psychological treatment interventions such as critical incident stress debriefing (Mitchell & Everly, 2000). I maintain that for groups such as the military, after-action group debriefings, properly timed and conducted and focused on events rather than emotions and reactions, can have great therapeutic value for many participants by helping them to place potentially traumatizing events in a broader context of positive meaning (Bartone, 1997).

REFERENCES

Allport, G. W. (1985). The historical background of social psychology. In G. Lindzey & E. Aronson (Eds.), *Handbook of social psychology* (3rd ed., Vol. 1, pp. 1–46). New York: Random House.

Bartone, P. T. (1989). Predictors of stress-related illness in city bus drivers. *Journal of Occupational Medicine, 31,* 657–663.

Bartone, P. T. (1993, June). *Psychosocial predictors of soldier adjustment to combat stress.* Paper presented at the Third European Conference on Traumatic Stress, Bergen, Norway.

Bartone, P. T. (1995, July). *A short hardiness scale.* Paper presented at the annual convention of the American Psychological Society, New York.

Bartone, P. T. (1996, August). *Stress and hardiness in U.S. peacekeeping soldiers.* Paper presented at the annual convention of the American Psychological Association, Toronto, Ontario, Canada.

Bartone, P. T. (1997). Einsatzorientierte Nachbesprechung (Debriefing): Was jeder militärische Führer wissen sollte [Event-oriented debriefing following military operations: What every leader should know]. In T. Sporner (Ed.), *Streßbewältigung und Psychotraumatologie im UN- und humanitären Hilfseinsatz* (pp. 126–133). Bonn, Germany: Beta Verlag.

Bartone, P. T. (1999a). Hardiness protects against war-related stress in Army reserve forces. *Consulting Psychology Journal, 51,* 72–82.

Bartone, P. T. (1999b, November). *Personality hardiness as a predictor of officer cadet leadership performance.* Paper presented at the International Military Testing Association Meeting, Monterey, CA.

Bartone, P. T. (2000). Hardiness as a resiliency factor for United States forces in the Gulf War. In J. M. Violanti, D. Paton, & C. Dunning (Eds.), *Posttraumatic stress intervention: Challenges, issues, and perspectives* (pp. 115–133). Springfield, IL: Thomas.

Bartone, P. T. (2001, June). *Psychosocial stressors in future military operations.* Paper presented at the Cantigny Conference Series on Future of Armed Conflict, Wheaton, IL.

Bartone, P. T., Adler, A. B., & Vaitkus, M. A. (1998). Dimensions of psychological stress in peacekeeping operations. *Military Medicine, 163,* 587–593.

Bartone, P. T., Johnsen, B. H., Eid, J., Brun, W., & Laberg, J. C. (2002). Factors influencing small unit cohesion in Norwegian Navy officer cadets. *Military Psychology, 14,* 1–22.

Bartone, P. T., & Snook, S. A. (2000, June). *Gender differences in predictors of leader performance over time.* Paper presented at the American Psychological Society convention, Miami, FL.

Bartone, P. T., Ursano, R. J., Wright, K. W., & Ingraham, L. H. (1989). The impact of a military air disaster on the health of assistance workers: A prospective study. *Journal of Nervous and Mental Disease, 177,* 317–328.

Bass, B. M. (1998). *Transformational leadership.* Mahwah, NJ: Lawrence Erlbaum Associates, Inc.

Bass, B. M., & Avolio, B. J. (1994). Introduction. In B. M. Bass & B. J. Avolio (Eds.), *Improving organizational effectiveness through transformational leadership* (pp. 1–9). Thousand Oaks, CA: Sage.

Bell, D. B., Bartone, J., Bartone, P. T., Schumm, W. R., & Gade, P. A. (1997). *USAREUR family support during Operation Joint Endeavor: Summary report* (ARI Special Rep. No. 34). Alexandria, VA: U.S. Army Research Institute for the Behavioral and Social Sciences. (DTIC No. AD-A339 016)

Berger, P. L., & Luckmann, T. (1966). *The social construction of reality.* Garden City, NY: Doubleday.

Binswanger, L. (1963). *Being in the world: Selected papers of Ludwig Binswanger.* New York: Basic Books.

Bonanno, G. A. (2004). Loss, trauma and human resilience: Have we underestimated the human capacity to thrive after extremely aversive events? *American Psychologist, 59,* 20–28.

Britt, T. W., Adler, A. B., & Bartone, P. T. (2001). Deriving benefits from stressful events: The role of engagement in meaningful work and hardiness. *Journal of Occupational Health Psychology, 6,* 53–63.

Burns, J. M. (1978). *Leadership.* New York: Harper & Row.

Castro, C., & Adler, A. (1999). OPTEMPO: Effects on soldier and unit readiness. *Parameters, 29,* 86–95.

Contrada, R. J. (1989). Type A behavior, personality hardiness, and cardiovascular responses to stress. *Journal of Personality and Social Psychology, 57,* 895–903.

Florian, V., Mikulincer, M., & Taubman, O. (1995). Does hardiness contribute to mental health during a stressful real life situation? The role of appraisal and coping. *Journal of Personality and Social Psychology, 68,* 687–695.

Frankl, V. (1960). *The doctor and the soul.* New York: Knopf.

Funk, S. C. (1992). Hardiness: A review of theory and research. *Health Psychology, 11,* 335–345.

Funk, S. C., & Houston, B. K. (1987). A critical analysis of the hardiness scale's validity and utility. *Journal of Personality and Social Psychology, 53,* 572–578.

Gal, R. (1987). Military leadership for the 1990s: Commitment-derived leadership. In L. Atwater & R. Penn (Eds.), *Military leadership: Traditions and future trends* (pp. 53–59). Annapolis, MD: U.S. Naval Academy.

Heidegger, M. (1986). *Being and time.* New York: HarperCollins.

Hoge, C. W., Castro, C. A., Messer, S. C., McGurk, D., Cotting, D. I., & Koffman, R. L. (2004). Combat duty in Iraq and Afghanistan, mental health problems, and barriers to care. *New England Journal of Medicine, 351,* 13–22.

Horowitz, M., Wilner, N., & Alvarez, W. (1979). Impact of Events Scale: A measure of subjective stress. *Psychosomatic Medicine, 41,* 209–218.

House, R. J. (1971). A path–goal theory of leader effectiveness. *Administrative Science Quarterly, 16,* 321–339.

House, R. J. (1996). Path–goal theory of leadership: Lessons, legacy, and a reformulated theory. *Leadership Quarterly, 7,* 323–352.

House, R. J., & Mitchell, T. R. (1974). Path–goal theory of leadership. *Contemporary Business, 3,* 81–98.

Ingraham, L. H., & Manning, F. J. (1981). Cohesion: Who needs it, what is it and how do we get it to them? *Military Review, 61,* 3–12.

Janis, I. (1982). *Groupthink* (2nd ed.). Boston: Houghton-Mifflin.

Jones, E., Woolven, R., Durodie, W., & Wessely, S. (2004). Public panic and morale: A reassessment of civilian reactions during the Blitz and World War 2. *Journal of Social History, 17,* 463–479.

Kirkland, F. R., Bartone, P. T., & Marlowe, D. H. (1993). Commanders' priorities and psychological readiness. *Armed Forces and Society, 19,* 579–598.

Kobasa, S. C. (1979). Stressful life events, personality, and health: An inquiry into hardiness. *Journal of Personality and Social Psychology, 37,* 1–11.

Kobasa, S. C., Maddi, S. R., & Kahn, S. (1982). Hardiness and health: A prospective study. *Journal of Personality and Social Psychology, 42,* 168–177.

Maddi, S. R. (1967). The existential neurosis. *Journal of Abnormal Psychology, 72,* 311–325.

Maddi, S. R., & Kobasa, S. C. (1984). *The hardy executive.* Homewood, IL: Dow Jones-Irwin.

Milan, L. M., Bourne, D. M., Zazanis, M. M., & Bartone, P. T. (2002). *Measures collected on the USMA class of 1998 as part of the Baseline Officer Longitudinal Data Set (BOLDS)* (ARI Tech. Rep. No. 1127). Alexandria, VA: U.S. Army Research Institute for the Behavioral and Social Sciences.

Mitchell, J. T., & Everly, G. S. (2000). Critical incident stress management and critical incident stress debriefing: Evolutions, effects, and outcomes. In B. Raphael & J. P. Wilson (Eds.), *Psychological debriefing: Theory, practice and evidence* (pp. 71–90). Cambridge, England: Cambridge University Press.

National Institute of Mental Health. (2002). *Mental health and mass violence: Evidence-based early psychological intervention for victims/survivors of mass violence. A workshop to reach consensus on best practices* (NIH Publication No. 02–5138). Washington, DC: U.S. Government Printing Office.

Paton, D. (1997). Managing work-related psychological trauma: An organizational psychology of response and recovery. *Australian Psychologist, 32,* 46–55.

Ritchie, E. C., Leavitt, F., & Hanish, S. (2006). The mental health response to the 9/11 attack on the Pentagon. In Y. Neria, R. Gross, R. Marshall, & E. Susser (Eds.), *9/11: Mental health in the wake of a terrorist attack.* New York: Cambridge University Press.

Roth, D. L., Wiebe, D. J., Fillingim, R. B., & Shay, K. A. (1989). Life events, fitness, hardiness, and health: A simultaneous analysis of proposed stress-resistance effects. *Journal of Personality and Social Psychology, 57,* 136–142.

Sinclair, R. R., & Tetrick, L. E. (2000). Implications of item wording for hardiness structure, relation with neuroticism, and stress buffering. *Journal of Research in Personality, 34,* 1–25.

U.S. Corps of Cadets. (1995). *Leadership evaluation and developmental ratings* (USCC Regulation No. 623–1). West Point, NY: U.S. Military Academy.

van Emmerik, A. A., Kamphuis, J. H., Hulsbosch, A. M., & Emmelkamp, P. M. (2002). Single session debriefing after psychological trauma: A metaanalysis. *Lancet, 360,* 766–771.

Watson, P. J., Ritchie, E. C., Demer, J., Bartone, P., & Pfefferbaum, B. J. (2006). Improving resilience trajectories following mass violence and disaster. In E. C. Ritchie, P. J. Watson, & M. J. Friedman (Eds.), *Interventions following mass violence and disaster* (pp. 37–53). New York: Guilford.

Weik, K. E. (1995). *Sensemaking in organizations.* Thousand Oaks, CA: Sage.

Weisaeth, L., & Sund, A. (1982). Psychiatric problems in UNIFIL and the UN-soldier's stress syndrome. *International Review of Army, Air Force and Navy Medical Service, 55,* 109–116.

Wessely, S. (2005). Victimhood and resilience. *New England Journal of Medicine, 353,* 548–550.

Westman, M. (1990). The relationship between stress and performance: The moderating effect of hardiness. *Human Performance, 3,* 141–155.

Wiebe, D. J. (1991). Hardiness and stress moderation: A test of proposed mechanisms. *Journal of Personality and Social Psychology, 60,* 89–99.

www.ingramcontent.com/pod-product-compliance
Ingram Content Group UK Ltd.
Pitfield, Milton Keynes, MK11 3LW, UK
UKHW020428010325
455677UK00029B/1063